A Hamster Is Missing

in Washington, D.C.

by ED SPIVEY JR.

A Hamster is Missing in Washington D.C.

Copyright © 2009 by Ed Spivey Jr. and *Sojourners* magazine

First Edition, October 2009
ISBN 978-0-578-03739-4
Printed in the United States of America

Cover illustration by Darryl Brown

Ordering information:
Visit store.sojo.net or call 1-800-714-7474.

Printed on recycled paper.

For Mr. Walker

Appreciations

I would like to thank the following people for making this book possible, even though—and few authors admit this, particularly on the appreciations page—I did most of the work myself.

Michael Curry, who was the first person to encourage me to compile my writings in book form. He bugged me about it for a couple years, so in return he gets the first order form for his own copy. (Note: shipping and handling are extra.)

Beloved wife Tricia, who believed in me, and told me to hurry and finish because there's vacuuming.

Daughters Colleen and Kate, whose laughter kept me on track.

Sojourners magazine founder Jim Wallis, for hiring me 35 years ago and letting me do pretty much whatever I wanted at the magazine.

Sojourners magazine editor Jim Rice, who stepped in and said that, actually, I *couldn't* do whatever I wanted, but it was okay for me to pretend.

And lastly, my parents, who have for many years saved a space on their coffee table for this book.

Medical Warning: This book was written at a facility where peanuts were consumed. They were delicious.

Contents

Introduction

An introduction is an important part of any book. It contains the pages that college students like to skip over, giving them an immediate sense that they are progressing nicely through their reading assignment since they are already on, like, page 15. (Unfortunately for the college students, it's usually the introduction that reveals Dostoyevsky wrote the whole thing in a brothel over a long weekend, which will be on the final.)

But it would be a mistake to ignore this introduction, because in it I have placed clues, intricately woven into the text, of a fortune of incalculable wealth, hidden somewhere in the nation's capitol. To find the treasure you must first read every word of this introduction, then carefully compare it with the introductions of 10 other copies that you have purchased. By meticulous cross-checking you will eventually discover a pattern, a map, if you will, that leads to an ancient trunk, bursting with gold and jewels. (Hint: It's somewhere under the White House, BUT THAT'S ALL I'M SAYING RIGHT NOW!)

BE THAT AS IT MAY, this project began with the modest goal of publishing a book that my grandchildren would one day read or, short of that, sit on while eating at the big people table. I'm gratified that interest in this book has become somewhat wider than my immediate family, and pleased that you have chosen a copy of your own, which hopefully arrived undamaged from the cheapest type of surface shipping we could find. (They left it squeezed between the screen and the door frame? Sorry.)

Regardless, just bend it back straight and begin reading what amounts to an extremely one-sided view of the past decade or so, a decade you might rather forget. Yes, there are some who insist that the fetid corpse of history is best left alone, and the rancid sweep of events that created our present misery best forgotten. But enough about raising my two daughters. This book is also about politics, which has its own categories of fetid and rancid, though using those terms to describe Dick Cheney is not a very nice thing to do and I won't stand for it. Besides, it's important to look closely at the past, because those who fail to learn the lessons of history are doomed to do poorly on a pop quiz given on the subject.

Hence (or possibly thus) reading the following essays can be an instructive exercise to shed light on particular events that, at the time, we couldn't believe were really happening. ("What? George Bush WON the election?! No way!" and "What? George Bush won AGAIN?! This is a joke, right?")

It may be painful, but let us start the healing process that will once and for all lance the swollen boil of our denial so that the green pus of truth can run freely into the sterile gauze of acceptance. And then maybe a nurse will help clean up, because this sounds really disgusting. ■

Author's Note

150 Years of Keeping the Faith

Oh, sorry, I meant to say 150 *columns* for Sojourners Magazine, which form the basis of this book. One hundred fifty years is another thing entirely. For example, it was a little more than 150 years ago that Dr. William T.G. Morton, a Boston dentist, used ether as an anesthetic in surgery. Before that, the chemical had been used mainly as a party gag. ("Hey, come over here and stick me with that bumbershoot. No really, I won't feel a thing, hah hah! ") It's just a pity that something discovered in 1275 by Spanish alchemist Raymundus Lullus wasn't put into standard surgical practice for another 600 years.

[Tee hee.]

I love doing that. Using lots of names and historical dates and mathematical calculations that copy editors have to painstakingly fact check, not to mention having to confirm the spelling of words like "anesthetic" and "Raymundus." They hate that. Especially since their usual editing technique with my copy is to hold their noses, set aside any shred of journalist standards, and pass it on. It's a good system and it works.

Fortunately, you won't read these essays for historical facts or 19th-century colloquialisms for umbrella (You were wondering what a "bumbershoot" was, weren't you?). No, you picked up this book to get away from tedious and unnecessary things like "depth" and "analysis" and revel in the false assumptions and wild conjecture that are my trademarks. Not to mention funny anecdotes about my daughters. (The early 20s is *such* a cute age.)

It's a proven formula that has entertained literally dozens of readers across the globe and won awards too numerous and embarrassingly obscure to mention.

For more than any other reason, you'll appreciate this book for its unwavering commitment to intellectual superficiality, something to which many of today's authors are surprisingly averse. When it comes to commenting on the important political and social issues of the day, I choose to live on the surface, like a water spider, only with fewer legs. Also, I don't feed on smaller insects and waterborne organisms, having once had a bad experience at a restaurant with that theme.

So opposed am I to using real facts that, if I told you that right after the first Gulf war then-Secretary of Defense Dick Cheney opposed a plan to invade Baghdad because it would leave us in a "quagmire," you would tilt your head back and laugh heartily in disbelief. But it's true (I checked myself, something that I'm loath to do), and with truth like that...well, maybe it's better just to miss the point altogether. Actually, that's kind of my motto, and it's the force---if an allergic reaction to anything of grave importance could actually be called a "force"--- that drives this book.

NOTE TO THE READER: In this book you may also find references to a topic that I like to call "religion," a subject that may be a little uncomfortable for some of you, unless you have accepted Jesus Christ as your personal Lord and Savior, in which case, you have nothing to worry about. If not, then in the short time you have left before burning in the eternal fires of hell, this might be a good distraction. ■

Apologetic Note (just in case)

This book is a compilation of two decades of writing in— and about—the nation's capitol. While the essays have been revised and updated using state-of-the-art copy editing techniques—such as spell-check, redundancy check, and spell check—time did not permit the author to re-confirm the status of many of the public figures who are subjects of his commentary. Some may no longer be with us, having been sent on extended fact-finding missions inside federal penal institutions. And others may be in that big Grand Jury Hearing in the Sky.

Naturally, good taste and common courtesy would suggest that the deceased should no longer be subject to award-winning satire. Sadly, such is not the case. I mean, we're sorry they're dead and all, but the truth cannot be buried or silenced. (Nor, for that matter, cremated and spread movingly over the blue waters of the ocean or, depending on wind direction, the new deck shoes of grieving family members.)

No. The author's comments remain unchanged, and *will* stand the test of time.

Sorry, Strom and Jesse. Miss you. ∎

Democracy in Action
(what, again?)

August, 2000

(Editor's note: The following contains misstatements, factual errors, and gross generalizations, such as the reference that many Congressmen are secretly in league with Satan. Satan emphatically denies this.)

As Americans prepare for the next election—mainly by turning off their televisions and hiding in the tool shed until December—what's needed is a fresh perspective on the coming political storm. As a long-time resident of the nation's capital, I'm in the perfect position to convey some of the little-known truths about our complicated political process, such as the fact that every member of Congress belongs to a devil-worshipping cult.

See, that's the kind of information you don't get from your local newspaper, and not just because the editor is afraid that federally deputized monkeys will fly down and carry him off, even though that only happened once.

It's hard enough for Americans to keep tabs on their elected officials, since years ago the government constructed the Capital Beltway, a road system designed to ensure that people driving to Washington, D.C., end up in, like, Pittsburgh.)

Fortunately for you, I'm here inside the Beltway, breathing the same air as the politicians, drinking the same water, and experiencing the same stomach cramps immediately afterward (I think they need to change a filter or something).

In this critical election year, I'll be keeping my "eye on Washington" and reporting about the sights and sounds, the smells and textures of the incumbents' efforts to remain in power. In fact I'll cover ALL the senses, if I can just remember that other one.

I'll look under the dirty fingernails of this powerful nation and report on what I find here, and maybe even take some scrapings to send to the police since I saw that in a movie once, and they caught the killer, just from fingernail scrapings! It was really cool. I would never have thought to do that.

But then, I'm not a forensic scientist. I'm a reporter, keeping my "eye on Washington."

ONE OF MY IDEAS is to "shadow" a congressman or congresswoman (okay, congressman) to see how he or she prepares for re-election. When he was first elected, he was still full of hope and promise and hadn't found a bar yet. By now, of course, he will have forgotten about his constituents as he attempts to squeeze head-first into the briefcase of a rich lobbyist.

If I may digress, to me a newly elected member of Congress is like a person with a freshly purchased Big Mac. When they get to the table, it's all very tidy, the buns stacked uniformly on top of each other, the ingredients neatly ordered inside. Similarly, a new congressperson arrives at the "table" of Washington, D.C., with his expectations neatly stacked in anticipation of taking a "big bite" out of this town. Unfortunately, in a short time the mayonnaise of their hopes begins to ooze out and the two all-beef patties of reality begin to shift. And then the dreams of this congressperson's little sesame seed world begin to slip just like the pickles always do. Plus, their hands get all gooey.

And when he takes a breath—"steps back," if you will—and looks at the sad spectacle before him, he notices the colorful McDonald's placemat. He reflects for a moment on the little cartoon characters and the happy phrases in their word balloons. And then he wonders what it would be like if, instead of listening to other congressmen make long speeches, he could just read their word balloons. "There wouldn't be room for as many words, so we couldn't say as much," he says to himself, pleased that non-elected people would have taken much longer to reach this conclusion.

BUT BACK TO THE sandwich and the important metaphorical point I was making. The congressperson must decide, and decide quickly in this election year, whether to attempt to reassemble the Big Mac of his Washington career, or to just pick up the placemat and start licking the food off of it, briefly obscuring his head from nearby reporters. But in all honesty, wouldn't the latter choice be just giving in to the pressures that electoral politics places on Congress? Wouldn't that be taking the easy way out?

I can't answer that question. All I know is whenever I do the same thing with one of those placemats, I have to clean my glasses afterward.

Anyway, I hope this has been a useful look at this election year, providing some helpful insight for those of you who don't wake up in the most powerful city in the world like I do. But don't worry. I put my pants on the same way you do out in the hinterlands. (And then I have to take them off again since my shoes never fit through the legs. I always forget that.) ∎

First Dance

The global economy is in shambles, the presidency is in crisis, and Americans are struggling under the weight of a broken health care system. But hey, I've got my own problems. Our 12-year-old wants to go to a dance. With boys.

Forgive me if I tend to focus on personal experiences rather than commenting on important political and historical events. But I feel that the universal lessons are best drawn from one's own life, rather than, say, from public figures such as Trent Lott, who I think has plastic hair. (It never moves.)

Lately, the fundamental truth I've discovered is that when it comes to accepting the approaching adulthood of their children, most parents are clinically insane. Case in point: The invitation to the middle-school party arrived via the U.S. Mail and, by law, we couldn't open it or discard it without our daughter's knowledge. Silly law.

We knew this day would come, but we felt that she still needed a couple more decades at home before beginning her social life outside our double-locked front door. Our reasoning was as follows: She is a straight-A student, a disciplined athlete, and a warm, loving child. Naturally, once out of the house she would immediately take drugs, have sex, and join the Republican Party.

This is not about trust, we patiently explained to her as we declined to give our permission. It's about paranoia. Deep, creeping paranoia that parents get when a child reaches the teen-age years at the same time, coincidentally, that parents become quivering lunatics.

"Wouldn't you rather stay home and watch The Little Mermaid again?" I beseeched her, forgetting for the moment how odd I look when I beseech. But she wasn't interested. Desperate for a solid moral footing, I revealed that she is, in fact, a Southern Baptist and that God doesn't want her to dance. I would have quoted scripture supporting that point of view, but most dance references in the Bible are—can you believe it?—fairly positive.

In a related parentally-crazed act, her best friend had already been given permission to attend the dance and they were hoping to go together. This weakened my argument considerably. A flurry of phone calls between our two households revealed that both sets of parents were in misery. "How could this be happening so soon!? They're only 12 and some of the boys there may be AS OLD AS 13!"

I finally settled on a compromise: My daughter could lock herself in her room and play with her pets and we'd bring up ice cream later. This got me nowhere. "Oh, all right, you can go," we relented, "but a parent will chaperone and you have to come home an hour before the dance is over" (just in case she starts to have fun, we reasoned).

Fine, she said.

It was agreed that I'd represent the four parents, which was okay with me since I figured I could dance the whole time with my daughter anyway. (I could teach her "The Twist." Who wouldn't want to learn that?) We arrived in front of her best friend's house, and she joined my daughter in the back seat. The other dad walked up and simply said, "How's it going?" which is parent code for, "I trust you are prepared to do anything, including acts of extreme violence, to protect these two young girls from...uhm...whatever." I nodded, took a deep breath, and drove off.

Safely en route, it was now my daughter's turn to set the rules. I would let them out before we got to the school entrance. I would not walk them in. After I parked the car, I would count to 1,000 before entering the dance. When I came in, I would not look at them and I would not talk to them. Was that clear? Was I confused about any of these instructions?

We arrived and I let them out behind a large tree, so that when they stepped into the lights of the entrance it was as if they had just beamed down (from the Bad Parent Planet). After parking the car I counted to a little less than 1,000 (three) and ran for the door, steeling myself for the unknown indignities from which I would rescue my daughter. Already I could feel my hands on the shoulders of some 13-year-old boy whose vilest intentions I would unashamedly interrupt.

THE SCENE I BEHELD was shocking. It was not what I had expected. Actually, to the rational mind, it was exactly what one would expect of 12-year-olds: All the girls were on one side of the room, all the boys were on the other side. No intermingling, no acknowledging, no anything. Nothing frightful to be seen, except for the middle-aged man standing at the door red-faced and panting from sprinting a hundred yards in the record time of 48 years. How could I have been so wrong?

There were groups of bright, engaging young girls talking and laughing comfortably together. They were a credit to their species. The boys, on the other hand, were of a slightly lower order. Ants, maybe. In constant goofy motion, the boys surged back and forth past the dignified islands of girls. Their arms seemed to flail at random, like antennae, as they moved in search of...what? A sense of purpose? An opening line? A Gameboy?

The boys paused periodically in the snack area to rake up handfuls of pretzels. They ate a couple, tossed a couple, and dropped one in the punch bowl. "Hah!" they blurted out, quickly reaching the outer edge of their wit. The girls, of course, were not eating. They might miss some conversation, which was mainly on two topics: school and the DJ across the room, dreadlocked and all grown up—and very good looking. Mercifully (for me), his girlfriend sat with him.

I quickly realized that I was unnecessary in that place. In fact, being in the presence of those bright young people brought out many contradictory feelings, but mainly 1) I'm going bald, and 2) I'm guessing nobody wants me to teach them "The Twist." ∎

The Choice

October, 2000

In just a few short weeks you'll wake up on a crisp Tuesday after the first Monday in November and do your part to dramatically affect the course of history. That's the day you forget all about the election when you discover your mortgage check sitting behind the toaster, and it's already a week late (and possibly a little dark and crispy). So you'll frantically rush to the post office to send the bill by overnight mail, which will be delivered within the next calendar week, unless you express the slightest irritation at having waited in line for an hour. (Then your envelope would go in to the "special box.")

After all that, you will probably remember something about the democratic process and your civic duty to make your voice heard in the presidential election. In a moment of poignancy, you'll recall the impassioned belief of our forefathers that even a single vote can make a difference. And then you'll laugh and laugh, because of course a single vote doesn't make a difference, silly!

But what the heck, you're already up and dressed anyway. Plus, you don't want to make up some story to your co-workers about how crowded the polls may or may not have been, depending on whether you did or did not vote, and then, on that basis, have them accuse you of making up the whole story just to take off work. (Are you following this?)

So you'll go to a nearby school or fire station, walking by the colorful placards comparing the candidates to Winston Churchill and Mother Teresa, and then you'll vote for the persons best qualified to do the job. Unfortunately, those people aren't listed, because they were constitutionally prevented from running since they're not rich. (The reason being, the founding fathers were all pretty rich themselves, not including Benjamin Franklin who, while not wealthy, was the only signer who had prescription glasses and could actually read what he was signing. One can't help but wonder, then, why he didn't catch all those typos in the Constitution: you know, the "f"s that should have been "s"es, things like that.

(Historical aside: Franklin's main qualification as an official forefather was the fact that he was a forefather many times over, a feat accomplished by dating numerous foremothers.)

But what really matters in all this is that voting is so darn fun. It's the only time you get to use that cool hole punch thingy. I usually don't like any of the candidates, so I just punch holes by all their names. It may take a little longer, and it most certainly nullifies your ballot. But if you don't have any of thoase plastic packing bubbles, it's two minutes of tactile fun you just can't beat it.

DURING THE ACTUAL voting process—for reasons unknown and possibly sinister—when you stand in the booth only your legs will show. We think this is done because:

- Poll officers want to see your legs. It's just something they like to do and we probably shouldn't talk about it anymore.

- If your legs are visible officials will know when you start dancing. Then they can tell you to stop.

- The U.S. Census Bureau figures it can tabulate the number of people who vote by counting their legs, and then dividing by two.

AS A PATRIOTIC BONUS, when you leave the polling area a kindly senior citizen will pin a "I Just Gave Blood" button on your shirt, which means one of two things: He is in the wrong place, and if you think he's going to take his medication then you're just barking up the wrong tree, mister!

Or you were in the wrong place. This confusion can easily be resolved by asking yourself if you just woke up on the floor from a dead faint (that always happens when I try to give blood) or by removing your shirt to check for a little Red Cross Band-Aid. At this point, if you are wrestled to the ground by police then you probably just voted.

But if you take your vote seriously, and of course you do, then you eventually will have to suffer the consequences of your actions. For the next four years you will regret having voted for one of the following:

- President Al Gore. Tall, dark, and boring. The Monotone-In-Chief; the man who invented the environment; the candidate who caused an entire nation to cry out, "How can somebody so darn handsome and smart make me want to take a nap when he talks?!" Gore campaigned on a promise of continuing the Clinton legacy, except for that one thing.

- President George W. Bush. The man elected on a simple campaign slogan: "Don't let the fact that I've done nothing my entire life keep you from electing me to the highest office in the land. (Was that a good read? Did I do okay? Should I have come down a little softer on that 'nothing' part?)"

Actually, for a time, Bush's well-funded campaign was in a political quandary around that Elian Gonzalez business, when it was discovered that he was a child, illegally. On the one hand, Bush's individual rights credentials were well-served when he criticized the Clinton Justice Department's daring pre-dawn raid. On the other hand, during the seizure of Elian, guns were brandished, which, according to Bush, "is good, right? I mean, we like guns, don't we...? Or are we against that? Where the heck are those note cards with my talking points? ...Anybody?" And it's that kind of fast thinking and oratorical acumen that assured Bush the presidency. But only if the debates were cancelled.

And, of course,

- Pat Buchanan of the Reform Party.

...Who?

Yes, the new president will have much to contribute to the new century. And it will be all your fault. ∎

Raising Kids
with Minimal Hamster Loss

I t started with a silence, not a noise. The kind of silence that makes a parent sit bolt upright in his bed; an unnatural awakening, a feeling of...something wrong. It was 3 a.m. when I got up to check on the girls, but they were sleeping comfortably, as evidenced by the fact that they were both completely tangled in their sheets, heads dangling over the edge of beds and arms splayed in painful angles across their faces. In short, at peace. No indications of the tragic drama that had just occurred.

What had awakened me was the absence of the usual nocturnal scratching that our pet rodent made, that annoying chewing and scratching that once scared the life out of me when I was up late under the covers reading Jurassic Park by flashlight: "The velociraptor approached almost silently, the only noise coming from the click of its central claw on the floor...."

Scritch... scritch...

I didn't realize the sound was from the hamster in the next room until I'd already leapt into the closet, yelling back to my wife, "THERE'S SOMETHING HORRIBLE IN THE HOUSE! GO GET THE KIDS WHILE I WAIT IN HERE!"

But no noise tonight, and that could mean only one thing. (Well actually, two things, if you count the fact that my wife's

"Learn French While You Sleep" tape had stopped. Why? Je ne sais pas.) The silence meant the hamster had escaped. And there it was: an empty cage with the door askew. And dangling from the side was a crude little rope made of tiny hamster sheets tied together.

In the morning we would go through the tearful motions of searching for the errant rodent. But I knew the odds were against us. You see, we have cats. Smart, very alert cats. My kids call them "Blackie" and "Whitey," but on the street they go by "Black-E" and "Why T." Tough cats. Not the kind of cats who'd catch a hamster and just give it a good talking to before putting it back in its cage.

It's hard to know whom to blame in these situations. But senators Ted Stevens(R-Alaska) and Mitch McConnell (R-Hades) live in the same town as us, so I think I'll blame them. But seriously, it's difficult to comfort young girls with a loss like this. Boys, one assumes, would mourn for a short time, perhaps a second, then say, "Okay, let's go get another one." We don't have boys because of that, and also because boys eventually become teen-agers and my wife says that we already have one male adolescent in the house, although I don't know who she means.

For a while parents can say things like "Oh, Petey will be back, I'm sure. Maybe he just went for a walk." But eventually the truth becomes obvious, even to little girls: Cats are hideous, untamable, and opportunistic creatures who just lie in wait for that day when, like in that old movie, *Honey, I Shrunk the Kids,* we'll shrink to the size of small rodents and then they'll eat US, too, which a dog would never do, and that's why we should have got a dog in the first place, like I wanted. But we got cats instead, which still bugs me. I mean, the worst a dog would do to us, if we were to shrink like in that movie, would be to lick us with his giant dog tongue, which would be gross, I admit, but then we could ride him over to the house of a brilliant scientist who could put everything back to where it was.

This may seem far-fetched. But don't think for a minute that cats aren't thinking in those terms. They saw the movie, too. And they loved it. ∎

Electoral Shock

January 2001

(Editor's note: The following includes a grossly unfair mocking of the rules our founding fathers used to create the Electoral College, which guaranteed that rural colonies would have the same rights as urban colonies. Of course, in the late 1700s there really weren't any urban colonies. New York City was an intersection. Chicago was a French trading post. (Trapper: This croissant smells funny. It's muskrat, isn't it? Be honest, you put muskrat meat in this croissant, didn't you? BasTARD!) And despite it being almost a century before organized athletic events, Philadelphia already had the meanest football fans in the country.)

At press time our nation hung in the balance. Evenly split between opposing sides, we waited to see what the outcome would be, and prayed that our divisiveness would somehow resolve into a clear choice between "Who Wants to be a Millionaire?" or "Survivor II."

Coincidentally, the presidential election had similar problems, which by now have all been worked out, resulting in the Oval Office being occupied by one of the following:

- a tickled George W. Bush ("Say, is this Corinthian leather?" Staff: "Sir, pay attention, please!")

- a confident Al Gore ("My first priority is to kiss my wife." Staff: "Actually, that's no longer necessary, Mr. President.")

- or, and I speak with the hope of an entire nation, it could be...Alexander Haig ("I TOLD you I was in charge!")

As I write this, vote counters in Florida are still painstakingly tabulating—in many cases, by hand—the numerous flecks of vitriol spewing from the mouth of Republican spokesman James Baker. Additionally, officials in at least six Florida counties have been unable to account for the mysterious loss of several inches of height from Democratic spokesman Warren Christopher.

The fear, of course, is that no matter who wins the presidency, he will be ineffective in leading a bitterly partisan Congress unable to achieve anything of significance. No wait. That was last year.

THIS WHOLE ELECTORAL MESS was, in my opinion, caused by the state of Florida which, geographically speaking, has always been the one kid in class who'll do anything to get attention. While the other states nestle closely together in relative harmony, Florida sticks its leg out, looking like a complete doofus trying to touch the equator. ("Look, everybody! I can almost reach it!") Let's face it, Florida is the unwanted uvula of the continental United States, the little hangy-down part of our electoral discontent.

And the people in Florida are no help, since most don't even know how they got there. Take my parents, for example. Just a few years ago they were happy in their nice little home in southern Indiana, mom in the kitchen baking treats, dad in the backyard innocently firing his air rifle at the neighbor's cat. And then one evening, large unmarked vans from the AARP pulled up, shoved them and their belongings inside, and forcibly relocated them to Florida. (Presumably, the AARP has done this to reduce mailing costs).

Of course, not every senior in Florida is to blame for the

mismarked ballots and other voting irregularities that turned this nation's presidential election into what the founders never envisioned: something really interesting.

Nope. It was my dad's fault.

He admitted as much during his weekly phone call reminding me how much money he spent to raise me. On election day he accidentally wandered into a polling place thinking it was the starter's hut at the golf course. After looking for a foursome, he picked up a ballot and, anticipating another good day on the links, scribbled down his score for the front nine and dropped it in the ballot box. This caused a chain reaction whereby many seniors assumed they needed to write their golf scores or their blood pressure levels in the little squares to the right of Al Gore's name. Unless they voted for Buchanan, in which case they just filled in the little devil face.

And the rest is history. Or is it geography?

In fairness, that kind of random, forgetful behavior is my father's only fault. At age 77, he is still taller, stronger, and decidedly better looking than me, and he takes great pleasure in shaking my hand so firmly that I'm forced, once again, to flee into the comforting arms of my mother, while he taunts me from the next room: "Well, there goes MOMMA'S BOY again! Hahahahaha!" Granted, this hasn't happened in more than a year, and I feel I've grown up a lot since then.

But back to this voting thing. The real problem is that the election was held without Super Soakers or badminton rackets, devices that I would have enjoyed seeing Al Gore and George W. Bush use against each other, or at least on James Carville. In fact, if politicians swatting each other were a varsity sport at the Electoral College, maybe more students would enroll there and it might get noticed more than just once every four years. ■

Capitol Snowstorm

(Editor's note: Given the accelerated warming of our planet—which scientists have blamed mainly on George W. Bush's use of SUV's when clearing brush on his Texas ranch—you may be unaware of something called "snow," a meteorological phenomenon whereby small bits of frozen water fall on the ground, coating it with a pleasing whiteness. This used to occur during the period known as "winter," at a time before the year's seasons were called Early Summer, Late Summer, and Only Three More Months Until Early Summer. The following was written when a lot of "snow" fell during "winter.")

After finally digging out from the 27 inches of snow that fell on the nation's capital—a city founded on a simple democratic principle: "What's a snowplow?"—it's time to look back at the beauty of it all and appreciate what could only be described as a "winter wonderland." Or, maybe "house arrest."

Actually, being housebound for almost five days was a real gift to our family. It gave us an unexpected opportunity to enjoy being together and have the kind of intimate fellowship that families seldom experience. And for good reason. You go *nuts* with all that intimate fellowship.

It was the worst snow in 50 years. It was so bad that one radio station played the shower scene music from *Psycho* during weather forecasts. And Washington's mayor was not reassuring when he announced his strategy for dealing with the blizzard: "Wait for spring."

The snow made things even harder for the federal government, which was already closed by stalled budget negotiations. Fortunately, because of a generous contribution from the National Rifle Association, the House of Representatives was able to remain open.

To be honest, the blizzard had its good points. We've been waiting years to go sledding, for example, and I'd forgotten how much fun it is to rush down a hill on a soft bed of fresh snow for a few yards before separating from your sled, then sliding the rest of the way down on your stomach, scooping a cubic yard of snow down your neck. Fortunately, I was wearing extra layers, which immediately turn the snow into ice water on your bare skin. I'd forgotten how much fun that is. Which is why we only did it once. (We stopped because I was using up too much Chapstick on my chest.)

THERE ARE a lot of fun things to do when you're stuck inside the house. For example, I got to teach my daughters "Crazy 8s," a card game from my childhood that gave me hours and hours of laugh-out-loud fun.

Not interested. Instead they taught me *their* card games: strange, brutal games like "Scum," "Frog Juice," and "Spit," which entails a frenzy of drawing and discarding in a race to see who can be the first to slap their hands violently down on the table.

Amiable father: Can I play this card here?

Daughters, laughing condescendingly: Sure, Dad. But then... WE GET TO DO THIS! [Slap! Slap! Slap!]

Who taught them these games? Satan?

Being cooped up for a week, I also learned important social lessons from my wife, who helpfully pointed out: "No, I'm not retaining water. I'm wearing EVERY SWEATER I OWN! Now turn up the heat or I'm going to start burning stuff for heat!"

Speaking of grumpy, our cats also hated being stuck in the house. Naturally, they prefer to be outdoors, where every day offers new experiences, challenges, and adventures, which they totally miss, of course, because all they do is sleep on the porch.

But during the blizzard, Blackie and Whitey mainly sat by the kitchen window and stared out at the bird feeder. While dozens of plump little birds flitted back and forth, the cats drooled, quivered, and frequently thumbed through their copy of the *Audubon Field Guide to Flying Snacks*. (*Whitey:* "Ooh, yummy. Look that one up." *Blackie:* "Let's see. Purple Finch. Slightly tangy flavor. Serves one."

BUT, IN ALL MODESTY, I'm a good man to have around in a snow emergency. I know just what to do: Start panicking about milk.

"But you don't drink milk. And we've got two gallons in the fridge," said my wife, obviously at the breaking point. I tried to calm her down by reassuring her: "WE'VE GOT TO HAVE MILK! WE'LL DIE IN HERE IF WE DON'T HAVE MILK! AND WE'RE OUT OF THOSE LITTLE BATHROOM CUPS, TOO. WE'LL NEVER MAKE IT!"

Obviously, we were reaching the end of our rope. ("OH NO! WE'RE OUT OF ROPE!!") It's like that when you're snowed in. You're reduced to primal instincts. You revert to the time of prehistoric cavepersons, when people spent their day hunting wooly mammoths and hoarding toilet paper. ("OH NO! WE'RE OUT OF THOSE WOODEN POINTY THINGIES... WHADYA CALL THEM?" *"Arrows."* "WE'LL NEVER MAKE IT THROUGH THE WINTER!" *"It's spring."* "WHATEVER!")

So I bravely struggled to our snow-bound car (or, as we called it, the "large white mound out front"). I had my shovels, the tire chains, and the tire chain instructions.

STEP ONE: Determine if your car is front-wheel or rear-wheel drive.

STEP TWO: You haven't the faintest idea, do you?

STEP THREE: Take instructions inside and have spouse explain it.

OK, so I hitched a ride. What's the big deal? Anyway, I get to the store and it's London, 1943. Empty shelves everywhere. People pushing, yelling, getting angry. And just because I removed a few items from their carts. In one store, all four meat coolers were completely empty except for a dozen packages of beef tongue, roughly two pounds each of pinkish, cellophane-wrapped cow muscle. ("Hey kids, guess what we're having tonight? Give up? ...It's TONGUE!") Actually, just the sight of a cow tongue was enough to make me stop eating meat. (It's also enough to make you stop smoking, gambling, cursing, burping out loud, spitting in public, and claiming false deductions on my taxes. Not that I would ever do such a thing). I'm telling you, one look at a beef tongue and you *know* the fear of the Lord.

At the hardware store, on another foolish trip out of the house, I asked the cashier why the snow removal crystals cost $27.50 for a 10-pound bag. In a fit of honesty, she replied: "It's simple. We're gouging." Doesn't a blizzard just bring out the best in people?

And I haven't even talked about the surprise meal the kids tried to make us. ("Mom, Dad, don't worry about the smoke alarm. We're broiling something for you. By the way, snow removal crystals are the same as salt, right?") ∎

Dateline: Our Nation's Capital

(Editor's note: The following was written shortly after the at-tacks on 9/11. If you think it was too soon to find humor at this traumatic time, then you probably don't have monthly writing deadlines and editors who insist that there be at least a shred of currency to your silly little columns. The fact that this won first place in a national humor writing contest...well, we're just sayin.)

Those of you in the hinterlands—when you're not tak-ing care of your hinter—are probably wondering what life is like now in Washington, D.C., the nation's capital, the most powerful city in the world, or as Pentagon officials have helpfully pointed out, a "target-rich environment."

Well, there's one thing that's true: We're sure as heck not scared! Nope, Washington, D.C., is getting back to normal. Peo-ple are going to work, shopping, eating out, and pretty much doing what they always did. At least, I think they are. It's hard to tell, since I'm crouched here under my desk and hoping my mommy calls.

But seriously, with a few exceptions, our lives are really no different than yours. We still put our pants on one leg at a time, after checking for booby traps. We still shop for life's staples: milk, eggs, gas mask filters. And, like you, we still have the freedom to just get in our cars and drive anywhere we want, the only difference being we never actually get there, on account of the Humvees. And the soldiers who, under strict orders not to use racial profiling, are stopping everybody who doesn't look like a member of the Osmond family.

The reasons are clear, of course, as law enforcement officers continue to search for followers of the man who has distorted religion for his own devious purposes, the man whose adherents are even now living and working among us—possibly even next door to you—waiting for instructions from this twisted usurper who makes a mockery of God.

But enough about Pat Robertson. Let's get back to life in our nation's capital, a town that has the "can do" attitude to come together in a crisis and, in unison, pee in our pants whenever a car backfires.

What's more, even the tourists are returning to Washington, secure in the knowledge that every step they take is being monitored by armed men with telescopic sights. So I say "Enjoy yourselves, Mr. and Mrs. Tourist!" And don't worry. After a couple of hours you'll get used to walking around with your hands in the air. (Repeat after me: "Nice soldiers.")

THE OTHER NIGHT, after dropping off my daughter and a friend at a local movie theater (where, I assume, they had planned to meditate on our national crisis), I was stopped at a military roadblock and asked where I was coming from. I thought it rather an odd question, but I patiently explained that the roots of my beliefs were first forged in the Southern Baptist church of my youth, but how lately I have been incorporating the liturgical rituals of Catholicism, thus deepening my.... "Move on," he interrupted, and rather brusquely, I might add. I briefly considered giving him a good talking to, but I demurred, if that's the word I'm looking for, after seeing his largish sidearm and the similarly accessorized personnel behind him.

Security is so tight here that if Jesus himself returned in all his glory, he wouldn't get very far (since he's of Middle Eastern descent). His legions of angels—with lyre and harp—would have to wait around in the parking lot until officials finally released him, after realizing he has a Hispanic name.

Biological warfare has been the latest fear here in Washington, with the newsweeklies running frightening covers about the dangers of anthrax and other viral threats. Turns out, however, that the best protection is for citizens to just stop reading newsweeklies until they return to their usual coverage of more important topics, such as Jennifer Lopez' wardrobe.

But we don't want to minimize the threat that these viruses pose, since treatment admittedly involves painful visits to an HMO (which researchers have linked to prolonged and unnecessary suffering in the waiting room). In an effort to help Americans avoid exposure to these harmful substances, the federal government has issued the following simple instructions:

- Stop licking the envelopes and boxes your mail comes in. It might have been okay before, but it's just not a good idea now.

- If you get a package containing a white powdery substance, don't immediately empty it into a glass of water and drink it. It's understandable that you'd want to do that, but not recommended.

- When you first come in to work, don't lick your keyboard. This time-tested practice of checking for yesterday's donut crumbs is, unfortunately, just too risky now. ■

Beep Beep

(Editor's note: This piece was written after U.S. troops first coun-ter-attacked Afghanistan after 9/11. Some of the observations may seem less accurate now, such as the reference to the "re-building the country," which should have included "except New Orleans and parts of Mississippi, not including the casinos.)

A s Afghanistan's newly appointed leaders gather to rebuild their nation, we are confident that a last-ing peace will endure for, oh, at least a week or two. Forgive my lack of confidence, but let's face it, when most of the guys in charge have the word "warlord" on their business cards, it gives us pause. Afghans themselves are taking a wait-and-see—formerly, wince-and-cower—attitude since their new leaders look suspiciously like some of the folks that, on a daily basis, used to poke them with sticks and ask with a beard-enhanced brusqueness, "Why aren't you in church?"

"Tribal leader" is another phrase you hear a little too often over there, and it's not very reassuring when it shows up on a politician's résumé. It means that, at a meeting to decide what the nation should export besides shrapnel wounds, one of the new guys could whip out a Kalashnikov and demand a bigger cubicle. (For those of you who, like me, once thought Kalash-nikov was the respected Russian playwright who penned "The Cherry Something," that's why you got a "C" on your college literature test. The correct answer, of course, is Chekov, which everybody else got right. Unless you were sitting next to future president George W. Bush, who at that moment was distracted by the fact that if he didn't return the empty kegs by 3 p.m. his fraternity would lose its deposit money. When he did finally answer the question, he wrote "Mr. Spock" who everyone knows is WAY smarter than that Chekov dude.)

But what was I saying?

Oh yes, my George Will-like commentary on the war in Afghanistan (or, as FOX News refers to it, "AMERICA AT WAR!") [flecks of saliva added for emphasis].

Not to name names, but the guy we're most worried about in the new government is Mohammed "You Talkin' to ME?" Fahim. He was appointed defense minister since it would be an easy transition from his previous job: ruthless killer. But that's one of the problems you have in a country where "road improvement" means putting down more land mines: Most of the top guys are thugs. And it goes without saying that you can't ask the women to help out, because all they'd do is promote education and human rights and pretty soon you've got rampant human dignity and, trust me, that's NO way to lead a nation back to the Middle Ages.

In fairness, the head of Afghanistan's new government, Hamid Karzai, is a respected negotiator, and he speaks fluent English. And as any American can tell you, being foreign and speaking English is the best way to cultivate America's trust, since our diplomats don't have to talk loudly to be understood. So it's that much easier to get down to the business of nation-building, especially the part where we loan them money for bombs and infrastructure development. But mainly bombs.

THE GOOD news, of course, is that the Taliban is on the run, Osama bin Laden has that real tired look of a guy working double overnights at the Stop 'n' Shop, and al Qaeda's reign of terror has been reduced to a pony-tailed drifter with a pair of Acme Exploding Shoes. (And, as any kid knows, this never once worked for Wile E. Coyote, no matter how many times he tried. In related news, federal air marshals preoccupied with inspecting an elderly woman's knitting bag failed to notice two suspicious men boarding a flight to Atlanta, one carrying a large boulder-flinging catapult and another man with a giant rocket tied to his back. Neither made it on board, however, since both somehow managed to fall off a cliff before reaching the aircraft.)

But the point is, the modern world is finally winning out in Afghanistan. Just days after Kabul was freed, men were able to shave their beards and for the first time in years taste the sweet fruits of freedom, which, for your average Afghanistan guy, is the ability to purchase posters of Indian movie stars. Who knew? (Hey, I don't make up the news, I just report it.) And women, who for the past five years were forced to remain indoors, cook and clean, and keep their heads covered, were able to finally show their faces outside. But then they had to go back home and cook and clean. And put up their husbands' new posters. ∎

Les French

When we sent our oldest daughter to France last year in an exchange program we got excited about what we might get, you know, in exchange: perhaps some good cheese, or fine wine, or maybe one of those really ugly French luxury cars (the ones that look like giant slugs, only less stylish).

But what appeared on our doorstep this summer was none of these things. It was a French kid. A French teen-ager, to be precise, who expected to live with us for the same amount of time that our daughter spent with her. (Apparently she didn't understand that giving is much better than receiving.)

But who could blame a foreign-type person for wanting to visit the most powerful, most advanced nation in the world? In fact, she spent much of the first day wide-eyed and speechless, at least until I stopped driving on the sidewalk. (I was in a hurry, and I was careful.) Coincidentally, one of her first cultural lessons was the unique way American drivers interpret traffic lights. I patiently explained that in our country green means "go," yellow means "also go," and red means that drivers curse loudly to themselves: "Dag! I'd better hurry through this intersection because some other cars will probably be coming from the other direction!"

Knowing that the first few hours with a new family and a different language could be uncomfortable, we tried to set our guest at ease by asking questions that any typical 13-year-old could answer: Who is your favorite rock singer? What kinds of foods do you like? Why does your government sell weapons of mass destruction to Iran?

I personally enjoyed interacting with this child, and took it upon myself to acquaint her with the privileges and perks our family enjoys in this, the richest nation on Earth. She was impressed when I told her that we generally spend vacations camping near a beach. She sadly replied that back home her family never camped, but was instead forced to spend summers at their ocean-front house. In Cannes.

When she mentioned that her favorite pastime is skiing, I quickly bragged about the nearby hills of Pennsylvania where the best of manufactured snow provides hours of picturesque, slightly downhill fun.

Again, a clearly disappointed child lamented that she had never skied on human-made snow, since her family lives about an hour from the Alps. They get a lot of real snow there.

But what most set our guest at ease was my own fluency in French, since I took the language in college. (In fact, I can still remember how to use raison d'etre in a sentence: Non, non! Je ne desire pas les raisins avec mon d'etre. Translation: No, thank you. I don't want raisins with my d'etre. Almonds, maybe. But definitely not raisins.)

I never hesitated to use my French whenever I thought it would be helpful to the child: "Would you like to be toast this morning?" I asked her one day. And later: "Tonight for dinner I have made the delicious shoes and Wednesdays."

And I'm sure she was grateful before a long car trip to be reminded to "go through the bathroom."

Like any lover of language, I also added to my French vocabulary whenever I could. After a day of shopping, our guest was showing me some of her souvenirs and I excitedly blurted out, "Hey, what's the French word for 'souvenir?"

"Souvenir."

"Oh."

Actually, we were never that concerned about the language barrier since, having spent last summer in France, our own daughter should be pretty fluent, right?

Dad, to French girl: "Don't you just love this cheese? In America we think fromage is best served in these little flat orange squares, individually wrapped, of course, for our protection."

French kid, looking to Colleen for help with the difficult words (such as "near-cheese by-product"): "Pardon?"

Colleen, patiently translating: "Do yew lak zee cheez?"

It's comforting to know that after three weeks of language and cultural immersion in a foreign country, our daughter can now speak English with a very good French accent. (She also brought back a swell Eiffel Tower key ring that was made in China.)

The children learned a lot from our guest, who brought a new level of politeness and decorum to the dinner table. It was refreshing, for example, to hear a child say a simple "no, thank you" when offered food, instead of the more traditional American reply, where the child shakes her head violently, clutches her stomach, and makes loud retching noises in the direction of the floor.

But the most important lesson we learned from our young ward was how to eat salad. Apparently, the French are taught at an early age to use a knife and fork in meticulous coordination. With salad this means carefully pushing every side of a leaf of lettuce onto the fork until what you're putting in your mouth is this neat little vegetable packet. No mess at all. In my house we simply fork up a piece of lettuce roughly the size of a newspaper page and shovel it in, temporarily obscuring our entire heads in the process. This makes French people laugh, we found out.

They also stare disapprovingly when Americans talk with their mouths full. I didn't realize we did that until I happened to glance over at a disgusted French child watching me using spaghetti as a second language:

Dad: "Did you minmflughtoktch?"

Daughter #1: "Mmphlogathinch."

Daughter #2: "Naglollgunch?"

Dad: "Ha ha ha ha!" [Burp.]

Despite these fundamental cultural differences, we learned that people of all nationalities can get along. In fact, our young guest invited our whole family to visit her in France. She said we have to eat on the porch. ∎

Robert Mugabe: Nobel Laureate? Maybe Not.

August, 2002

(Editor's note: This piece was originally written describing the 2002 disputed presidential election of Zimbabwe's president-for-life Robert Mugabe. Since that time, Mugabe has won additional rigged elections and has generally made his country a great place to live and work, if you are one of Mugabe's heavily-armed henchpersons—literally, "persons of hench." For the rest of Kenyans, it's pretty much a living hell. Given that, it's no wonder Mugabe missed receiving the Nobel Peace Prize, but only by just THIS much.)

Some readers have complained that my writing has become too personal, too focused on my being a great father, an award-winning art director, and a god-like figure to the rest of my office colleagues. In response to this concern, I have decided to look beyond my personal preoccupations and devote this entire commentary to international events, and the surprising way these events remind me of my own life. Such as when Zimbabwe's president Robert Mugabe recently stole the election and then wondered why foreign observers were "making such a big deal about it." Coincidentally, these were the exact words my daughter used when she came in after curfew.

In fairness to Mugabe, he simply wanted to spare his people the trauma Americans suffered after our own disputed presidential election, a time of acrimony and mistrust that turned brother against brother, sister against sister, and first cousin against third cousin twice removed. (That one got ugly). Mercifully, Americans have the attention span of one of those squirrels that carefully buries nuts in the yard and then says to himself, seconds later, "Whoa! Somebody buried some nuts here! Well, too bad for them, 'cause it's finders keepers!" So Americans pretty much forgot about that election, unless they weren't Republicans from Florida.

But in Mugabe's case, he simply cancelled the recount, declared himself the winner, and jailed his opponent for treason. Republican strategists in our own coutry are looking at this technique, though reportedly the National Rifle Association will not support it unless handguns are used in the process.

Mugabe wisely reasoned that a recount would have taken up valuable resources from his cash-strapped country, resources that could better serve the needs of his people by being directly deposited into his secret Swiss bank accounts. (Or is it Swedish bank accounts? I'm always confused about that, which probably explains why, when I recently wired millions of dollars overseas, I got the money back with a nice note pointing out that, while they appreciated my amusing postscript, their hills were not, in fact, alive with the sound of music, since that's Austria.)

Sadly, Zimbabwe's constitution stipulates that this may be the final term for the aging patriarch. But Mugabe staffers are confident that the supreme court can find a loophole, particularly if one of the justices were dangled upside down out the window of a high-rise office building. "Oh yes," the judge would say as he watched his pocket change fall to the concrete several stories below, "I'm *sure* there is a reasonable way to satisfy all parties concerned. Can I come back in now?"

President Mugabe is proud of his decades of achievement and was recently honored with a commemorative bumper sticker: "You think this is bad? Honk if you'd rather live in Rwanda."

BUT WHY WOULD I associate Robert Mugabe with my youngest daughter and her curfew violation? I know it's unfair to compare a brutal dictator to a teen-ager, since many brutal dictators go on to live decent and productive lives. And to be honest, it must be said that there are clear differences between the two. For example, unlike Zimbabwe's president, my daughter would never hire armed thugs to get her way, since she seems to do just fine without them.

The bottom line here is that when Mugabe comes home late he doesn't have to explain why. Whereas, I have LOTS of questions for my daughter. Fortunately for her, she had a good excuse: "I was having too much fun to come home."

This is only one of the annoyances of sharing a home with a ruthless dictator...excuse me, a delightful teen-ager. Sadly, even our pets suffer the consequences. For example, all of our food is tested on animals. Some think this cruel, but it's the only way my daughter feels safe consuming the meals we prepare for her. At our home, the nightly ritual of suspicion and investigation begins with saying grace—which the cat respects by quietly licking her private parts until we're done—then she reaches up and pulls the tablecloth half-way down onto my daughter's lap to review the evening's fare. Unfortunately, the cat is almost always disappointed, since we're basically vegetarian (except for bacon. Oh yes...bacon.).

Our daughter watches warily as she feeds the feline small portions of the food groups. Only after the cat has survived each course will she consider eating it herself, an obstinacy similar, I'm sure, to Robert Mugabe's own refusal to hold free and fair elections. Let's face it, in Zimbabwe the "balanced diet" of justice not being served at the "dinner table" of his authoritarianism. Plus, the "loud belch" of his decades-long dictatorship is embarrassing to the dinner guests.

Whether Mugabe has a cat, however, is unknown—he seems more like a big-dog kind of guy—and it's probably none of my business, except to observe that I wouldn't want to meow distractingly during an important meeting to discuss Zimbabwe's principle export, which, and I'm guessing here, is definitely not democracy. ∎

Dog Poop Park

Morning in Washington, D.C. A time of high energy and even higher expectations as powerful people rush to do powerful things, their hands firmly gripping a leather briefcase, a steaming cup of fresh coffee, and sometimes, dog poop.

Surprised? Well, I guess it is a little risky to be rushing around with hot coffee in your hands, since you could spill it all over your power tie. What's that? Oh, it was the *other* thing that seemed a little odd.

Actually it's a common occurrence in the Capitol Hill neighborhood where my youngest child attends school.

Every morning we drive by Dog Poop Park–that's what we call it–and observe the half dozen or so Washingtonians exercising their pets. "Exercising" is the polite Capitol Hill word for "letting them poop," since that seems to be the main concern of the dogs. (Although, in fairness to the dogs, that's actually not all they do. They also run around in circles.)

Now, before you point out that this violates a number of local ordinances and telephone the mayor so he can immediately dispatch city inspectors as soon as he gets back from a fact-finding trip to some other continent, let me inform you that this is one of the cleanest parks in the city. The conscientious dog owners are very meticulous about tidying up afterward. They follow the dogs around, some even in their pajamas. (The people, not the dogs. Although once there was this cute little terrier wearing the same sweater that a co-worker wanted to buy from a catalog until I told her it didn't look all that good on the dog. It had horizontal stripes and made her hips look a bit large. The dog's, not my co-worker's.)

Anyway, the people carry these wads of paper towels with which to immediately dispose of the evidence in a nearby trash can. Which I think is great, because it keeps the parks clean. (But then, I'm not the guy who empties the trash cans which, after a couple days, probably start to cook up like a Mississippi compost heap in July.)

My daughter and I have become so fascinated by this Washington phenomenon that one day we pulled over to watch. The people all know each other, it seems, and there is much laughter and sharing of views. While the dogs do their "business"– and then carefully inspect each other's "business"–the owners chat and sip from coffee mugs they've brought from their nearby homes. As I said, some are still in their pajamas, and we watched one woman in a colorful bathrobe holding a steaming mug in one hand and gesturing enthusiastically with her other hand. Her other hand contained dog poop.

Granted, it was wrapped in a paper towel, but as she walked the few yards to the trash can she clearly wanted to get her point across. And who could argue with this woman, what with her dog poop hand gesturing directly at the man with whom she was speaking. He listened intently, nodding frequently, though careful to stay clear of her non-coffee-mug hand.

This behavior seemed perfectly acceptable to the people in that park. Each had probably used this gesturing technique many times. Heck, some of them are probably lawyers and have done this in court.

Prosecutor: "Objection! Your Honor, the attorney is badgering the witness with dog poop again.

Judge: Counsel will approach the bench, but NOT TOO CLOSE!

Eventually my daughter and I had to leave, so we didn't see the end of this daily ritual in the park. Presumably, the friends called their dogs and walked back to their homes, exchanging warm goodbyes and promises to phone later. But probably no hugs.

THIS REMINDS me of another anecdote related to this genre, which we should get out of the way now, since heaven knows we don't need to revisit this topic.

Three of my friends who go climbing every spring found out a couple years ago that when nature calls on some mountains it's a collect call, since they now have to "collect" what they previously left behind. In technical mountain climber terms, this means you have to "bring your poop back down with you." (I can see you're getting a little uncomfortable with all these references to poop, so for the three people who are still reading this, why don't we just refer to it as...uhm... "rush limbaugh.")

So anyway, the 14,000-foot summit of Washington state's Mt. Rainier is a very popular climb. So popular that the Rush Limbaughs people were leaving behind began to accumulate noticeably in the cold temperatures prevent decomposition. Which is why the park rangers made the rule.

Mt. Rainier is a long climb. It takes a couple of days. You can't wait until you get back down to rush limbaugh.

So climbers have to take up these special plastic bags and these special plastic ties which, may I suggest, had better be extra strong plastic bags and darn good plastic ties. My friends tell me this practice changes the nature of the climb somewhat, although it does not alter the absolute thrill of looking out at the world from 14,000 feet, surveying the snow-covered ridges, breathing the crisp air, and, above all, avoiding the rhythmic sway of your companion's backpack.

Let's be honest, if there was any fun to mountain climbing before this new rule, well, it now includes a hugely un-fun thing. Not that I had to be discouraged from mountain climbing anyway, what with the cold, and the falling, and the frostbite, and the falling. But now that the guy stringing rope down to me could also have a leaky backpack... well, it makes me want to sit home and listen to the radio. But not Rush Limbaugh. ∎

Be afraid. Be very afraid. (It's the law.)

September, 2002

(Editor's note: The references to increased domestic surveillance are for historical purposes only. The federal government no longer spies on its own people. Right?)

Those of you just back from vacation might need a quick reminder about the state of the world. It's not good. But you wouldn't know that, would you, since you were away on that annual orgy of beach-related self-centeredness, ignoring our wounded planet and wallowing in the unearned privileges of the American leisure class.

I know I was.

Well, there's a lot more to be afraid of now that you're and the government is making darn sure we don't forget any of it. Turns out, over the past few months federal officials got a little lax in warning us about the many threats to our way of life, and I'm not just talking about the brain-dissolving toxins recently discovered emanating from Viagara commercials ("Viva *what?!*").

No, these are serious threats, the kind that make President Bush talk publicly about being "firm in our resolve" and "resolute in our strength" and "Hey, I had to cancel the barbecue because of this!"

Now the federal government is taking every threat seriously, and has ordered that citizens having a good day are to be immediately stopped and reminded that, at any moment, something really bad could happen! And—this is the important part—it wouldn't be the government's fault.

Paper cut? CIA: "Told you so."

Funny noise in the bathroom? FBI: "Made you look."

Tummy ache from that second tube of Pringles? Department of Homeland Security: "Hey, if you want to live life on a razor's edge like that, don't blame us."

AND IF THAT WASN'T ENOUGH, we're told that federal agents discovered a plot to detonate a dirty bomb in Washington, D.C. A "dirty bomb"—which, it's safe to say, will never be featured in Martha Stewart Living—is particularly dangerous, experts tell us, because it could release hundreds of Fox News crews on unsuspecting Americans and subsequently fill the airwaves with the kind of commentary that should only be viewed from under your bed. While holding your blankie.

Not to be outdone by the previous paragraph, government officials are quick to add that there are other really scary things that could be used against us, too, like car bombs and shoulder-fired missiles, although thank goodness neither of these is available in this country. Except at gun shows.

But don't worry, a terrorist can't just walk up and buy anything from gun seller (The Gun Seller Creed: "Look, it's none of my business"). First he has to wait out the five-day cooling off period, otherwise known as the "five days to work on your sinister plan." Hopefully by then federal SWAT teams would have already burst through the front door and forced the occupants to lay face down on the floor, at least until one of them finally said, "Excuse me, officers, but I think you want the wacko next door. He left earlier in an unmarked van full of fertilizer. But while you're here, would you mind bursting into his garage and getting my lawn mower back? I think it's in the corner behind the hand grenades he got off e-Bay."

But not to worry, these latest frightful announcements have unleashed one of the most powerful forces in our nation's arsenal of defense: Sunday morning talk shows. Every weekend, with dramatic music playing in the background (in case you forgot how important this stuff is) we watch such shows as "Meet the Press" and "This Week With Sam Donaldson's Eyebrows" (soon to be replaced by "This Week With George Stephanopoulos' Boyishly Rugged Jawline") where wealthy journalists ask wealthy political leaders about the fate of ordinary Americans, people that neither has actually met. There, in the "electronic marketplace of ideas," government representatives candidly reveal where they were when they first realized it was someone else's fault. It's a spirited "give and take" of ideas, with the seasoned journalists occasionally looking up from their Lexus accessories catalog to ask hard-hitting questions—the kind designed to make politicians squirm—such as, "Have you noticed how bad the valet parking has gotten downtown?"

It's freedom of the press in action, one of America's most cherished principles, and something the people of Iraq have never experienced. Which is why we should immediately send George Stephanopoulos over there to explain—with dramatic music playing in the background—why he gets paid so much for sitting in a chair on Sundays looking handsome. (And then he could explain why he has a "Osama Bin Laden Wears A Thong" T-shirt in his luggage, which we put there just for fun.) ∎

West Nile Virus

It's finally here. The dreaded West Nile Virus has made it all the way from the left side of that big river in Africa, and now we're listening for the tell-tale hum of mosquitoes struggling to stay aloft with the extra weight of their little disease backpacks. We don't know how the virus got here (one theory has it hiding in the wheel wells of a hedge fund's private jet returning from delivering bundles of cash to an offshore bank), but it's here now and it's nasty.

Apparently it preys first on the infirm, and it has afflicted a local man whose immune system was already weakened by chemotherapy. Our best wishes go out to him, as does our gratitude to the local media for keeping us informed about the threat. We particularly want to thank Fox News for its rare display of moderation in *not* starting its evening newscast with "GIANT DEATH MOSQUITO IN NORTHWEST D.C.! WE'LL TELL YOU HOW YOU CAN SURVIVE RIGHT AFTER SPORTS, WEATHER, AND AN INTERVIEW WITH THE THIRD RUNNER-UP ON *AMERICAN IDOL!*"

Unfortunately, the worst thing about the West Nile Virus is that it could be anthrax. Or, for that matter, the common cold. There's little difference in the first indications. Medical professionals have warned us to be on the lookout for "flu-like symptoms," but that could be anything, including—and I'm just guessing here—the flu. In fact, it could be just about *anything.* Got a headache? ("Hey, it's been nice knowing you.") Muscle aches? ("Dude, tough break. Can I have your stereo?") Watery eyes? ("GET THIS MAN TO A HOSPITAL!. Sigh. If ONLY he'd worn that beekeeper hat—-with matching safari cloak—- that I bought for him at Banana Republic!")

Why can't really scary diseases have really scary and obvious symptoms? After all, whooping cough gives you the whoops, right (I think)? So why can't the West Nile virus give you quivering pustules around your belly button, or maybe an extra finger growing out of your neck? There'd be absolutely NO risk of contagion since somebody like that would get his own subway car, even at rush hour. And no way he could mix into the singles bar scene downtown, once they found out he's not a lawyer.

And while we're at it, anthrax should give you whirling eyeballs and a high squeaky voice. And for that matter, Legionnaire's Disease should come with a Fez hat and an uncontrollable desire to ride around on little motorcycles. (or is that Shriner's Disease?)

As you can see, you can't tell a medical menace from a chest cold.

AMBULENCE DRIVER TO DOCTOR: This man was just bitten viciously by a rabid dog that wandered into a Wal-Mart!

DOCTOR: How can you tell?

AMBULENCE DRIVER: Well, they always have that big brown sign, and lots of cash registers...

DOCTOR: No, you moron! I mean how do know he's been bitten,?

AMBULENCE DRIVER: Oh, that. Well, he's got flu-like symptoms.

I guess I just miss the old days when a plague looked like a plague, and people pushed around wooden wheelbarrows full of stinking corpses, leaving no confusion about whether the sick needed a nasal spray or a backhoe. We may be getting to the point that the only thing medical schools need to teach is how to say "Yep, you've got flu-like symptoms. Beats me what that means. By the way, can I have your stereo? ∎

The Vice President's Check-Up

During the first term of the Bush administration, Vice President Dick Cheney's personal physician was abruptly relieved of his duties after it was learned that, for the past several years, he had been addicted to prescription medications. [So far, this is completely true.] This was not known at the time of the vice president's last physical.

And how are we doing today, Mr. Vice President? Well, I guess that's what we're here to find out, on account of, I'm the doctor, right? Am I right? Okay, please remove your clothing and step into this gown and we'll begin the examination. I realize you've done that already, but you did it before I asked you to, so we have to start over. Got to stick with the protocol. Once you start bending the rules...HEY, is it REALLY bright in here, or what!? Why do I have to walk into a room AND GET A HEADACHE, FOR CHRISSAKES?!! NOW WHERE'S THAT LIGHT SWITCH?!

Ahhh.

There, that's lot better, don't you think, Mr. Vice President? Darkness can be very soothing. Now let me just sit down over here for a minute and rest while you do some deep knee bends. That's just the thing to get your heart going while I review your charts. Course, I can't see your charts with the lights off., but I can use the beam from my otoscope, like one of those laser pointers.

Hey look at the ceiling, Mr. Vice President. I can make swirly lines. There's a figure eight.

Funny word, otoscope.

Orange is another funny word. Orange. It's sounds a lot like "aren't," don't you think? Just yesterday I asked somebody, like, "orange you glad you don't have cancer?" He laughed.

Maybe it wasn't cancer. I forget.

Hey, did you ever notice that "vice president" sounds a lot like "nice resident"? That's... that's...I'm sorry sir, I usually don't get so emotional during physical examinations. It's just that "nice resident" sounds so loving and tender, and...so touching, somehow.

Do you have a tissue? Oh, here's one.

Does this room feel hot to you, Mr. Vice President? Feels hot to me. I'm going to open that window. Damn, it's locked. Piece of crap window! WHY CAN'T I EVEN OPEN A FRIGGIN' WINDOW AROUND HERE?!

Well, the ears look good. Any other, what's the word, "symptoms," you're concerned about? How's the heart, I mean how does it feel when you put your hand over it? Can you feel it thumping? I call it thumping. Some doctors like to call it thrumping, but that's the same as thumping.

So let's have a listen. Where's the stethoscope. Have you seen my stethoscope, Mr. Vice President?

WHERE'S MY DAMN STETHOSCOPE!

Oh, here it is.

Now cough.

Good. Okay, now hum.

Excellent. Now go "ummmm budda budda budda, umm-mm budda budda budda."

Is it cold in here? *I'm* sure as hell cold. Like ice, I'm cold. Here, feel my hands, Mr. Vice President. Feel how cold they are.

Now let me look in your other ear. Hey, I'm having a whatayoucallit...deja vu...yeah, deja vu. Like I already looked at that ear. Okay, well let's look at the other ear. I mean IN the other ear. You really can't tell much from looking AT an ear. You have to look IN the ear. That's one of the first things I tell my students. Gotta look INSIDE things. THAT'S where the answers are.

Did I ask you to cough already?

Hey, is it hot in here, or what? I'm sweating like a...like a... like...

Like a....

Okay, well let's have a look at the prostate.

At this point Secret Service agents, summoned by muffled cursing from inside the examination room, burst in and subdued the Vice President, who was refusing to complete his physical, a procedure that is required by law. Cheney was quickly escorted out, however, when his doctor complained about the heat and grabbed an agent's service revolver with the intention of firing through a window to let in some fresh air, on account of it was really hot in there. ■

Children of the Damned,
The Sequel

(Editor's note: No one under 17 should be permitted to read the following item. Parental discretion advised.)

I t seemed like a good Idea; a cheerful, celebrative evening of Yuletide fun. Why not invite the children, we asked while planning the annual Christmas party for our small group. The kids can join in the hot cider and cookies, exchange home-made gifts, and experience the spirit of Christmas by singing with us the cherished carols of our heritage.

Wrong.

Because on the way to the party our kids must have been secretly kidnapped by aliens and replaced with...the Sacrilegious Children From Hell!

The evening progressed as planned, a little noisier than expected perhaps, but as we lit candles and gathered our families around the hearth a calm began to settle over us. What a great way to spend a holiday evening, we parents foolishly thought to ourselves.

"Let's sing 'Jingle Bells,' " I suggested to the gleeful giggles of our precious children. But midway through the song it happened: A single voice In the back of the room started to rise above the rest..."Jingle bells. Batman smells, Robin laid an egg..." And one by one the children began to join in, gradually drowning out the adults, chanting louder and louder..."Batmobile lost a wheel and Joker got away, hey!"

We all laughed. Cute kids, we thought, Incorrigible. But seriously, children, let's sing...oh..."Joy to the World." And we all joined in again. But soon, from the other side of the room, a different voice departed from the authorized lyrics with, "Joy to the world, the bus blew up, and all the kids are...." But this time the grownups tried to drown It out by singing louder, "...and wonders of His love, and wonders of His Love, and..." but these kids outnumbered us almost two to one, "...with a knife stuck in his head, a knife, a knife, stuck in his...."

The parents glanced suspiciously among ourselves trying to determine whose kid it was that taught this mockery to our dear ones (I know It wasn't *my* kids...) when another child suggested we sing "Deck the Halls."

A great Idea, Joshua. Now *that's* the kind of example we want our children to see. I nodded approvingly to his parents and strummed a chord on the guitar. But before I could sing the first verse Joshua stood up, a look of madness In his eyes, and led the children with "Deck the halls with gasoline, fa la la la la la la la, strike a match and watch it gleam, fa la la la la la la la la...." With a determined hunch of our shoulders, the parents sang out loudly, "Don we now our gay apparel..." but we were no match for the screaming horde and their forceful, "...aren't you glad we play with matches, fa la la la la la la la la...."

Remembering the first rule of good parenting ("separate the children"), grown-ups spread through the giddy pack, grabbing the impressionable youngest, placing them on our laps, and reaching for the older troublemakers to corral their energies.

"Let's not forget what Christmas Is all about," I said, unconvincingly. "So why don't we sing, 'We Three Kings.' " Hoping the Images of the manger and the long Journey of the Wise

Men would calm the unruly urchins, the parents waited for quiet, then solemnly began, "We three kings of Orient are..." "TRIED TO SMOKE A 10-FOOT CIGAR...." The dam was starting to break..."IT WAS LOADED, IT EXPLO-O-DED...." Who ARE these kids, anyway? "...No more kings of Orient are...."

Did they learn this stuff at school!? Is their home life so incomplete that it has to be filled with sacrilege? Is six hours a day of television too much? Should they be disciplined more regularly ("Stop singing or there'll be NO SECONDS ON DESSERT!")?

These and other questions ran through our minds as we hurriedly called an end to our festive first- and last-annual Christmas sing. We packed up our young embarrassments and began the short, merciful journey home.

Note: Only 15 more shopping days to remind your children they're not getting ANYTHING for Christmas. ∎

Safety First

October 2002

(Editor's note: Long before the Supreme Court's 2008 interpretation of the Second Amendment required mandatory handguns in every home, the District of Columbia had one of the strictest gun control measures in the nation. Writing for the Short-Sighted Revisionists—commonly known as The Majority—Justice Scalia said we can't have that any more. But BEFORE that, there were other attempts to take away our right not to bear arms.)

O ver the summer, an important initiative was launched to make our nation's capital an even safer place to live, depending on how quickly you can purchase a bullet-proof vest.

But, you may well ask in italics, doesn't Washington, D.C., already have nine separate police forces, as well as daily overflights by F-15 Eagles and armed helicopter gunships? Absolutely, I would reply from inside my home, since I seldom venture out and attract the attentions of armed helicopter gunships. (CO-PILOT: Hey, the guy in that backyard is either igniting a barbecue grill or a thermo-nuclear device! Should we call this in? PILOT: Nah. We'll handle it. Eat lead, possible terrorist!)

Given these considerable protections, it may seem surprising that Republican Sen. Orrin Hatch wants to ensure an even greater level of security by repealing Washington, D.C.'s 27-year-old ban on handguns, thus enabling citizens to "better protect themselves."

It's about time.

D.C.'s archaic gun law—barely enacted by an overwhelming majority of city voters—prevents a law-abiding D.C. resident from defending himself from an intruder who, in broad daylight and disguised as a possible mail carrier, might attempt to open his front door unannounced. The point is, citizens have a right to protect themselves from strangers who attempt to invade the sanctity of their homes or, in the case of Jehovah's Witnesses, their front porches.

(Facetiousness aside—but just for a moment—one day last summer I was quietly walking through the sanctity of my own home when I discovered Jehovah's Witnesses standing in my living room! It was a hot day, and a member of my family had foolishly assumed the New Testament imperative to welcome the stranger applies to EVERYBODY, even though Jesus clearly intended for there to be exceptions, Jehovah's Witnesses chief among them. After all, they are the pit bulls of unwanted conversation, never letting go of their unsolicited theological opinions until, exhausted, you finally relent and promise to read a Watchtower. Anyway, they had kindly been offered cool drinks to relieve the heat of the day and they wouldn't leave until, in desperation, I told them that the neighbor across the street had once asked me about the Godhead. They scrambled out the door like bloodhounds on the scent. Fortunately, after I sandbagged our front steps, they haven't returned.)

But back to

this gun controversy. Who better to understand the unique challenges of urban life than Orrin Hatch, senator from Utah, a sparsely populated rural state comprised mainly of Mormons, who are kind of like Jehovah's Witnesses, only with a bigger choir. Also, the senator resides in a D.C. suburb and travels by limousine, thus further informing him of what life is like on the dangerous, Starbucks-laden streets of our city.

In fairness, Hatch has little else to do these days since his main job in Congress—obstructing Clinton judicial nominees—doesn't apply anymore. Maybe the real reason the senator is thwarting the will of the electorate is because it offers a nice balance to his other pursuit: singing patriotic religious songs and selling them on his Web site. With songs like "Sweet Gentleness" and "Where the Marble Gardens Grow," he might need a gun or two to stop people from going "Ewww! Ewwwww!" whenever he walks by.

On second thought, maybe we should re-think the fact that most D.C. residents foolishly walk around without guns in their hands. After all, American soldiers allow each Iraqi family to have one assault rifle, so why can't I have one? Or a couple, for that matter. Although, I admit I haven't carried a weapon since my rubber band gun—a surprise birthday present—was summarily taken away from me. I had been using it as an instructive tool, patiently teaching squirrels to not climb on the bird feeder, when a meddling offspring noticed the hideous grin on my face and shouted, "DAD! You can't use a gun to SHOOT THINGS! It's not right!"

But I LIKE to shoot things, I should have replied, bringing logic to bear, and thus stating the strongest moral argument for gun ownership. After all, without guns one cannot shoot things, and where would that leave us? With squirrels and terrorists climbing on our bird feeders, that's where! So, I say, "Wake up, Washingtonians!" (also "FREEZE!" and "Come on, make my day!") and get the confidence and swagger that comes—free of charge—with every sidearm. After all, we can't expect the hard-working crews of helicopter gunships to solve all of our city's problems, can we? ■

In the Shadow of Self-Delusion

January, 2003

As our nation prepares for war against—depending on the mood of the president—al Qaeda, Iraq, or unnecessarily big words (such as "civil liberties"), it is a sober time in America, and that's a good thing. Serious times make for serious people, and in our nation's capital that means no longer "business as usual." For example, the halls of Congress used to be filled with pushy lobbyists passing out large amounts of cash and pressing their narrow agendas. But now when they do that, they wear those little American flag lapel pins. What a difference!

Yes, it's a new day in America, a time to recommit ourselves to the common good, a time to make the sacrifices called for in a time of war, and, above all, a time to move our cash into offshore accounts.

Of course, I'm not talking about regular people like you, because you don't have any cash. Nope, you foolishly put your savings into "fly-by-night" companies whose very names should have raised suspicions. Companies such as AT&T (Come on, spell it out! What are they trying to hide!), AOL-Time Warner (so, like, which is it?), and Johnson & Johnson (what, Smith & Smith wasn't available?) were among many companies whose stock prices are now lower than Jerry Springer's threshold of decency.

But we can't worry about our personal concerns now

because, as Secretary of Defense Donald Rumsfeld has emphasized, our nation is under the "shadow of war," and that changes everything. (Actually, "shadow of war" was the administration's second choice after "shadow of gargantuan self-delusion" was rejected because staffers felt it might undermine the president's ability to interrupt a meeting on, say, corporate malfeasance and suddenly blurt out, "Ooh, I know! Let's have a war!")

As we prepare for the inevitable confrontation with Iraq—or possibly North Korea—what we need are some inspiring words from someone who has recently overcome adversity and emerged victorious, with only a short prison sentence. Such as recently convicted former U.S. Rep. Jim "The Rug" Traficant, who spoke to the hearts of a nation when he proclaimed, "Hey, I don't CARE if my head looks like an exploding grain elevator, I'm innocent!"

Sorry, that's the most inspiring quote I could find from Capitol Hill, since congressional leaders have been too busy displaying their unity on the war. That way we won't notice they've done absolutely nothing on other, admittedly minor, issues such as health care, the environment, or what used to be known as the economy. It still *looks* like our old economy, but it doesn't quite have the zing that Federal Reserve Chair Alan "Mr. Party Hat" Greenspan would like.

I can joke about Alan—I call him "Alan"—since he's a personal friend of mine. The first time we met was in an optometrist's office several years ago. He came in to the waiting room and I immediately walked over to congratulate him on winning the Nobel Prize. I extended my hand and engaged in the following conversation, here rendered verbatim, far as I remember:

ME (with brash confidence): "You're Milton Friedman, aren't you?"

HIM: "No, I'm not."

ME (stubbornly): "Sure you are. You're Milton Friedman, the guy who won the Nobel Prize."

HIM: "I know who I am, young man. And I'm not Milton Friedman."

DOCTOR: "I can see you now, Mr. Greenspan."

ME (recovering nicely): "...uh...."

He may have forgotten that moving encounter in the years that mercifully intervened, but his memory may have been jolted awake at my oldest daughter's high school graduation when he and I ended up in the same reception line. Overcome with the emotion of our belated reunion, neither of us spoke or even looked at each other until my mother—she's from a small town and doesn't hobnob with celebrities like I do—asked if I'd take a picture of her and "Mr. Friedman." My mom, and the chair of the Federal Reserve Board, together at last.

I patiently explained that "you just don't DO that kind of thing in the nation's capitol," but she assured me it would be okay. Her plan was to walk up behind him while I framed the picture, then she'd bump into him, on purpose, but pretending it was an accident—in other words physically assault the Chairman of the Federal Reserve Board of the United States—and when he turned around made eye contact I'd snap the picture. Her friends back home would just assume she was having a genial conversation with the most powerful man in international finance. She also suggested I then immediately hand the camera to an identifiable passer-by just before bodyguards flung her AND me to the ground while Mr. Greenspan was hurriedly placed in a waiting limousine.

Fortunately, I distracted her with some of those little chicken sticks you find laid out at powerful Washington high school graduations, and we turned away leaving Mr. Greenspan alone to murmer a quiet prayer for God—any god, really—to smite us both down at the earliest possible convenience. ∎

Squirreling Away for Winter

With the importance that so many of us place on protecting our natural environment, I must preface my remarks about wanting to strangle the squirrel in my bedroom wall by first reassuring the reader that, at my office, I'm known as Mr. Nature. I consistently put the natural world before self, causing colleagues to see me as no less than a modern-day St. Francis. (Or maybe it's because sometimes I come to work in my bathrobe, on account of I forget.)

For me, there are no pro-environment laws too restrictive, no endangered species legislation too protective, no wetlands undeserving of care. Err on the side of Mother Nature, I always say, as I brake for crossing wind gusts. Paper or plastic? It's not a choice, it's an outrage!

That said, however, and with a clear understanding of the biblical call to care for God's creation, I want to wring that little squirrel's neck. I want to teach him a lesson that will say to squirrels everywhere that my home is not theirs to move into for the winter, as cozy as my home may be, compared to, say, a tree. As a general rule, I believe that undomesticated creatures, with the possible exception of Winnie the Pooh and Rush Limbaugh, should not live in houses.

Unfortunately, I have had little support on this matter from those of my own species. The other humans in the house—those whose side of the bed is not next to Grand Central Squirrel—have been taken in by said squirrel's bushy tail and cute expressions. They stand at the window and smile warmly as the animal scampers about, gathering leaves in its mouth and occasionally stopping, in a Kodak moment, to stand up on its furry little back legs and look directly at us. Then it scampers up the gutter spout and poops in our house.

To the rest of my family the cuteness of these moments outweighs any concern for my nightly discomfort, which leaves me coming down to breakfast with baggy eyes and a face gaunt from lack of sleep. (My looking like a jet-lagged Alan Greenspan obviously makes no difference to these squirrel-lovers.)

NIGHT AFTER NIGHT I am kept awake by the sounds of crinkling leaves as the squirrel wriggles in his makeshift bed, perhaps dreaming of a nut he once enjoyed. Or maybe some other nut.

I've tried to see things from the squirrel's perspective, and I imagine it's not easy settling in for the night. You know how it is when you're trying to get comfortable on a pile of dry leaves and fiberglass insulation. No matter how you shift your body, there's always a stem poking you in the ear, or scratchy fiberglass filaments creating a pre-cancerous irritation on your neck.

So my heart goes out to the little guy, and also my fist, as I pound on the wall trying to get him to stop whatever it is he's doing that sounds like somebody digging into a box of Cracker Jacks. (Which is hardly worth the effort these days, since the prize is just a piece of colored cardboard from China.)

Unfortunately, my wall-pounding seems to be making no difference, since the squirrel stops his movements only for a second, and probably says to himself, "There's that pounding again. Dag, some creature must have moved on the other side of that wall."

My plans to leave out poison or set traps have been vetoed by a family that insists on a more humane approach, one that I was similarly required to take some years ago when a mouse had nested under our bathroom sink.

It was a young mouse, too stupid to hide when we opened the cabinet door, and it would stand up on its little furry legs and sniff at us with interest. My daughters declared this Just The Cutest Thing and placed him under their official protection. Which meant I could neither poison nor squash it, leaving one of those catch-and-release traps as the only option. The mouse was easy to catch (being, as has been made clear, still young and stupid), but then the problem became "now what?" So I carried the trap to a vacant lot nearby and, with a motion that I had practiced beforehand, flung out the mouse at the exact moment I opened the little trap door. This was supposed to send the creature several feet away, where it could start a new life, possibly in the lucrative dumpster inspection industry. But my timing was off, and instead I flung the mouse straight down at my feet, where it quickly scurried for the closest dark space.

Which was up my pant leg.

I'd go into more detail but it STILL FREAKS ME OUT JUST THINKING ABOUT IT!

Not wanting to risk a similar incident with a squirrel, I've decided to just wait for spring, when warmer weather should send it outside. Then I plan to curl up on some leaves and fiberglass insulation and sleep until summer. ■

Bad Dog, Barney

March, 2003

(Editor's note: As our nation prepared to go to war against Iraq, only one writer that had the courage to stand up and report about the president's dog instead. And this is what he wrote.)

Remember the TV commercial where a man is walking down a dark city street and nervously glances back at two shadowy figures? The tension builds until the figures step into the light and reveal themselves as Boy Scouts, leaving the man visibly relieved—and a little embarrassed—that he'd completely misjudged the situation. Then the Boy Scouts beat the crap out of him and steal his wallet.

Okay, I made up that last part, because mental editing of TV commercials is what separates us from lower forms of life, such as Ann Coulter. But these days, walking down the street in fear seems a fitting metaphor for the times we live in, because at any moment a bunch of Boy Scouts could run up and beat the crap out of us. Although, again, that's just a metaphor, so it won't actually be Boy Scouts. They could be dressed like Boy Scouts, but then it would be a disguise and not a metaphor, so it's probably not relevant. But let's just move on.

IT'S A SCARY TIME. It seems like every rogue nation in the world (except Iraq) is developing nuclear weapons. The countries without nukes already have chemical and biological weapons (though fortunately none have been found in Iraq). And at last count, there were hundreds of al Qaeda operatives living secretly in our country (though probably none of them are from Iraq). Not to mention the fact that global terrorist networks are being financed by shadowy figures all over the Middle East (except in Iraq).

I think I finally understand why we're considering a pre-emptive strike against Iran: It's too late to be pre-emptive with anybody else. And if you can't be pre-emptive (literally, "when good guys shoot first"), you can't send in the military, right? Nope, you have to use (pronounce with a whiney sneer) the State Department instead—and let's face it, nobody's going to hang an American flag on his SUV for boring ol' [whining sneer again] diplomatic initiatives. Heck no! WAR brings a country together! And it's WAR that gives us a sense of common experience. (That, and regressive tax policies, deteriorating environmental protections, and an abysmally inequitable health care system.)

And then there's North Korea and its president, who looks like a Slobodan Milosevic celebrity Pez dispenser that got left in the car on a hot summer day (and is none too happy about it). Experts say what he wants—besides contact lenses in "today's hot colors!"—is simply a "place at the table." Just make sure the Beloved Leader doesn't sit next to the South Koreans since he'd probably snitch their dessert (or, as Kim Jong Il calls it, "Beloved Dessert").

So, as we approach this new season of war, it's important that the president have the full confidence and support of the American people, and not just the Electoral College. Because it is he alone who must assess the threats to our nation, and he alone who must make that lonely walk across the hall and ask Dick Cheney what to do.

THE WAR PREPARATIONS in the White House are intense—various pant legs rushing to and fro, and seldom a pat on the head to soothe things down. Of course, I'm talking about the only view of the White House that outsiders get nowadays: the Barney Cam, a camera attached to the First Dog's collar. It's the brainchild of the First Lady's office, which puts the pictures on the official White House Web site, thus providing a dog's-eye view of the places where history is being made. Or at least sniffed.

Barney travels from room to room, giving us a perspective of the White House that visitors seldom see, unless they're 14 inches tall, or perhaps crawling around on their stomachs hiding Enron files under the furniture.

Here's a picture of the elegant dining room, where dignitaries from all over the world never seem to drop anything good off their plates.

Here's the Oval Office, which has no corners, which is a good thing, since corners always seem to create this powerul temptation—like the sound of a rushing waterfall—to do something that is immensely satisfying to a dog, but which makes just people freak out and yell "bad dog!" at Barney. And there's that guy who sits around all day holding a briefcase hand-cuffed to his wrist. He hates it when Barney starts sniffing around. Plus, he never wants to play fetch with the "football."

There is much more for the American people to see, but right now Barney's anxiously looking for someone to let him outside, and they better do it quick because Barney was VERY THIRSTY earlier and doesn't much care if people are busy with war preparations because Barney really needs to go to the Rose Garden right now!

No Barney! Not on the vice president's secret papers! Bad dog. ∎

Batteries Included

I'm driving along the streets of Washington, D.C., dodging potholes recently sharpened and deepened by conscientious road crews, when it suddenly occurred to me that my lap was on fire. This doesn't happen much—in fact not at all—unless you count our family Advent ritual: Dad's yearly "Spilling of the Hot Cocoa" after cutting down a Christmas tree. It's a picture-postcard scene: the tree tied to the roof of the car, kids bundled against the brisk winter air, their faces wreathed in the warming steam from Mom's thermos, and Dad running around in circles yelling "EEECH! OOCH! IT'S HOT!" as a spilled cocoa stain spreads over his pant legs.

But this was not steam filling up the inside of my car. This was smoke. It was coming from my right pocket, which was also oozing burning liquid onto my leg (like in the movie Alien where somebody foolishly tries to cut off a tentacle from one of those little monster guys and this acid gunk gushes out and almost burns its way through the spaceship. It felt exactly like that, except Sigourney Weaver wasn't in my car to help me.

No stranger to crisis decision-making, I knew that quick thinking was required. In rapid-fire sequence my mind raced through the measures needed to resolve your typical burning pants emergency:

First: Buy new blue jeans. (No, wait! That probably comes later.)

First: Pull over, cursing loudly, and try to put out the fire.

Second: Ask forgiveness for cursing.

Third: Pull out burning contents of pocket and fling it on the floor, which I did, immediately burning my hand on an acid- dripping AA battery and a bunch of hot, smoking coins.

Apparently, I had missed the high school chemistry class where the teacher touched coins to both ends of a battery. (It might have been the same day I got such a bad haircut at lunchtime that I didn't go back to school. The vice principal later called this action "immature," "intolerable," and other things that I didn't hear because I was transfixed by the large facial mole that pulsated when he got mad.)

So anyway, I missed a science lesson that most of my class-mates have never forgotten, because it probably ended with the teacher standing beside a petri dish containing the smok-ing remains of a battery and saying: "People, never ever put batteries in your pocket. It would be bad." *This* class I had to miss? I never missed a day of geometry and I haven't used it once. Or, for that matter, English literature: "Never put the complete works of Shakespeare in your pocket. It might not burn, like a battery, but it's too big anyway.") You get the idea.

The battery was still smoking and crackling and I remem-bered reading once that batteries can sometimes explode. Not wanting the phrase "exploding batteries" to be mentioned during my eulogy, I gingerly scooped up the smoldering Dura-cell and tossed it out the window.

Crisis over. My adrenaline finally returned to normal levels and, as I sat there, a deep sense of peace spread through me. I knew that the hand of God had reached out and saved me from serious harm. (Of course, the other hand of God was stifling a big, God- sized laugh. The Almighty probably couldn't wait to go tell it on the mountain that I looked like a real doofus trying to find a parking space in the smoking section.)

When I recounted the experience back at the office, my colleagues were visibly concerned. OK, not at first. But after they stopped laughing they were visibly concerned.

Naturally, my family was more sympathetic. When I told the story at the dinner table that night, a look of anxiety crossed the face of my youngest child. I was deeply touched by Kate's reaction so I squeezed her little hand and assured her that daddy was OK.

"But Dad...you littered."

"Excuse me?"

"You littered, Dad. You threw the battery out the car window and you littered. It's trash and we've got to go back and find it, and dispose of it properly." Meanwhile, my supportive wife wondered out loud why she had apparently married Lucy Ball. (And then she asked if she should start taking bongo lessons and learn the Bosanova, just to keep up her end of the marriage.)

So the moral is: Don't keep batteries in your pocket. And if you forget and do anyway—since they just fit so perfectly in your pocket and, like spare change, come in handy at unexpected times—make sure you're close to a high school so you can pull over and run in for show-and-tell. But leave out the "tell" part when you get home. (Daughter: How was your day, daddy, and why are your pants just a smoking remnant of what they usually are? Me: I don't know, but it SURE wasn't from littering. ■

Goooood Morning, Iraq!

June, 2003

It's morning in Iraq, or, depending on your time zone, after-noon. Then again, it could be late at night, and you're won-dering where the day went. But back to our metaphor: A new day is dawning in the Middle East. Totalitarianism is over in Iraq, and the people will soon be experiencing the miracle of democracy which, studies show, is characterized mainly by high cholesterol and credit card debt.

Mercifully, the tyrannical personality cult has been van-quished and one man's maniacal hold on the populace is over. We don't know where he is, or whether he's alive or dead. We only know that Geraldo Rivera won't be bothering anybody again.

But most important, the United States has gained a pow-erful new foothold in the Middle East, something neighboring countries have long been clamoring for, with the exception of Iran, Saudi Arabia, Turkey, Yemen, Pakistan, Egypt, Turkey, and Qumar (no, wait, that's a fictitious country on TV's *West Wing*). Now that the United States has claimed victory, grate-ful citizens of the region have only one question for the Bush administration: "How come where we live is called the Middle East and where you live is called the West? Maybe YOU guys are in the East, and we're in the West. I mean, the earth is round, right? Heck, if you start with Guam, the Arab states are, like, in Hollywood or something."

Good points all. (Yeah, right, like John Wayne movies would ever be called "*Easterns!*") But to understand Iraq, and why it was necessary for our government to make up stuff and pretend there was a real reason to invade, we have to look back a little further than last week's episode of Survivor. (I know it's hard to turn off the television, America, but try to focus.) Sometimes, historical reflection is necessary.

IRAQ IS CONSIDERED by most Iraqis to be the Cradle of Civilization (not unlike how my hometown Indiana insists it is the Watermelon Capital of the World). Over the centuries Iraq underwent many changes, mainly the kind where people with the word "horde" on their vanity plates stopped on their way to the beach just long enough to set fire to everything that moved

Eventually, things settled down with the emergence of the Ottoman Empire, a powerful civilization of sophisticated and educated people who were known by their neighbors as "those know-it-all Ottomans." Impressed by the rich intellectual life of the region, Britain naturally felt something should be done about it, so they applied their time-tested diplomatic tool: the crushing heel of imperialism. (Note: British troops also burned everything that moved, but they weren't considered "hordes" because they wore nice uniforms.)

Already weakened by the precipitous crash of the ottoman market—19th century consumers had inexplicably switched to Stratoloungers—the Ottoman Empire was ultimately unable to repel the British army, and was quickly carved up into various smaller countries whose borders were determined by Britain's meticulous cartographical technique. (British mapmaker: "I know, I'll make it the same shape as me mum's Sunday hat!")

Enter America, and the promise Iraqis now have for freedom, democracy, and, in the not-too-distant future, maybe even tap water. (We're working on it.)

One Iraqi we talked to was ecstatic about the change of regime, and said he was particularly looking forward to getting a good health care system, with America's help:

IRAQI: Actually we had a health care system. A little short of medicine, maybe, but at least the health care was free.

US: Free health care? Dude, what planet are you from?! But don't worry, we'll set up an HMO right away.

IRAQI: That would be good. Then I can finally watch *The Sopranos*.

US: No, I said "HMO," which we have found is the best way to maintain the health of American corporate executives.

IRAQI: We don't have any executives.

US: Just be patient. In the meantime we're giving you the next best thing: jittery soldiers untrained in crowd control. No need to thank us, it's the least we could do.

IRAQI: [Sigh.] ■

Squish.
(Ugh. The Cicadas are Back)

I t's that special season again. The time when nature spreads its vociferous colors everywhere, igniting the world with the delicate striations of crimson and yellow, and the flaming tincture of auburn. It's a veritable explosion of color.

Or maybe it's just bug guts.

Whatever you call it, it's all over your windshield, because the cicadas are back and they're just as stupid as they were the last time. They're loud, they're ugly, and they like your head. And it doesn't help to shout "Look, I'm not a cicada!" or "but I barely know you!" When you're a cicada, the heart wants what the heart wants. Or is it the thorax?

These bugs shouldn't even be here, since they seem to defy Darwin's law of natural selection. They have no means of defense, no ability to hide, and they don't know danger when it's diving at them with wide open beaks. The phone lines in my neighborhood are sagging under the weight of birds who should have said "when" before they ate another one of those pudgy little casseroles with wings.

But you've got to feel sorry for the lowly cicadas. They gestate for 17 years, then emerge from the ground in search of nothing more than a little companionship, which they've got to find quickly, since they only live a couple weeks. Hardly enough time to enjoy the fullness of life: the brash risk-taking of youth, the challenges of adulthood, or the sweet reminiscences of old age. ("I remember last Tuesday. Now, those were the days.")

Nope. They dig their way to the surface and, like a college boy at Daytona Beach, desperately start searching for a mate. Same desperation, but without the beer. (My parents live near Daytona and are happy to report they rarely have to scrape college boys off their windshield, except occasionally in the spring.)

But can we really criticize the passionately hopeless behavior of cicadas? After all, they're going on reflex, not experience. For cicadas, there is no comunal body of knowledge to share, no oral history, no parental advice on how to live their short lives. For years the male lies alone in the ground thinking "I hope she likes me," not even knowing what she looks like. And they usually guess wrong. (One cicada thought a local woman's ear might be a good first date, which it wasn't, but the experience caused the woman to drive over a fire hydrant, disrupting water service to an entire neighborhood.)

Because cicadas lack the social structures of higher life forms, they miss out on the primary source of basic sex education: the sixth grade cafeteria.

TOMMY: ...and that's how it works.

BOBBY: No way.

TOMMY: Look, I heard it from a seventh grader, so it's gotta be true.

Without this kind of vital information sharing, cicadas are on their own, and from what I can hear, they only have one pick-up line (a high-pitched droning sound, which is SO lame). I figure if a cicada would say something different, like maybe "How's it goin'?" or even "Yo, Adrian," he would have a lot more luck than his peers.

BUT WITH OR WITHOUT romance, they all end up as lifeless lumps, most of them, it seems, in my back yard. When I walk outside it sounds like somebody chewing through a bowl of crunchy cereal, an observation I particularly enjoy making during breakfast with the family, some of whom are at that moment chewing on crunchy cereal. It's just one of the stimulus/response experiments I've been doing—for the sake of science—since the giant bugs have emerged.

I began conducting these experiments 17 years ago, when I first tested the reaction time of my young daughters by placing cicada shells on their shoulders, just outside their peripheral vision. While producing little in the way of usable empirical data, the resultant screams did cause me to hold my hand up to my face to keep from laughing out loud. (It was also good practice for denying culpability when said daughters told their mother a preposterous story about their father taunting them with dead cicadas. Such an imagination, these children.)

Repeating the same experiments today, 17 years later, with my control group having grown into educated, mature adults, I was interested to observe a similar reaction. As I watched, clipboard in hand to record the response to stimuli, daughters A and B ignored their preconditioning and screamed again. Then they again ran to their mother and I got in trouble. My consolation is in knowing that, like Galileo before me, we scientists are often least understood by those closest to us. ∎

Indiana's Finest

Being a resident of our country's last colony, Washington, D.C. ("Doesn't Count"), it's hard to approach this political season with anything but a jaded, albeit cynical, pessimism. Like most Iraqis, I am waiting for self-rule to be established in my hometown, and to experience "democracy," this new thing I keep hearing about where citizens have, like, a vote.

To compensate for not having representation in Congress, fortunately there are many benefits to living in the nation's capital, although I can't think of any right now because I'm too busy not drinking the water, which you shouldn't, on account of the lead, which there's too much of. (Of all the things I've taught my children, it's irony that I'm most proud of. For example, my youngest just came home from Central America, and when she got back to D.C. I had to warn her not to drink the water here.)

In the absence of meaningful political participation here, I have for years taken an interest in the congressional district of my youth in Indiana (motto: One Man, One Gun). I watch with jealousy as voters in my former district, after first receiving instructions from the Republican Party, exercise their right to vote. Hoosiers, as they are called—there's a story to that name, but it's really boring—are a devoutly conservative lot who, for example, believe the only foreign aid we give should be boatloads of bootstraps so recipients can pull themselves up by them, after paying for shipping.

The 8th District of Indiana, where I spent my formative years, is currently represented by Rep. John Hostettler, a fine Republican who was recently detained at an airport. Details are sketchy, so I'm not sure whether it was his laptop computer, his cell phone, or the loaded 9 mm semiautomatic handgun in his briefcase that caused concern among the security personnel.

In fairness to the congressman, who has a license to carry a concealed weapon, he had just come back from a visit with constituents in his district, or, as Washington insiders privately refer to it, "in-country," a frightening place populated by voters who foolishly make up their minds without first consulting a lobbyist.

Hostettler was cited on a misdemeanor charge of carrying a concealed deadly weapon. (Is it just me, or does the phrase "concealed deadly weapon" seem like an odd fit with the word "misdemeanor"?)

But let's not jump to conclusions. Rep. Hostettler might have stopped at a firing range on the way to the airport and, instead of tossing the gun into his car's back seat where it would be safe, perhaps he put it in his briefcase instead. Or maybe he felt that, in a time of increased citizen readiness against terror, he could provide back-up while on-board air marshals subdued a suspicious elderly woman. (You can hide a lot of stuff in orthopedic shoes.)

I tried to find out the real story, and left several messages with the congressman's communications director in Washington, but he hasn't called back. Without confirmation, we just don't know why the congressman was carrying that gun. Was it just an honest mistake that airport security personnel are still chuckling over? (You know what a great sense of humor those folks have.) Or was the congressman planning to rob a liquor store? Without official clarification this could be one of those stories the liberal media blow way out of proportion.

To be fair, the congressman is an avid sportsman, so it does make some sense for him to carry a pistol when he travels. After all, popping rabbits from the tarmac would really help pass the time when your plane is in line for takeoff. But as I said, his media guy hasn't called back and I just left another message, so I guess we'll never know if Rep. Hostettler is, in fact, a law-abiding man who is simply exercising his Second Amendment right to bear arms in a "well regulated militia," which the U.S. Supreme Court recently affirmed, particularly for Congress-men traveling on crowded airliners.

What we do know is that the congressman is from the same state as Dan Quayle, but I doubt there's any similarity. After all, I know Dan Quayle. I've made fun of him. And John Hostettler is no Dan Quayle.

TUM DE DUM...sigh. (Yes, I know the Dan Quayle thing was lame, but I'm just killing time here until the....Wait. He's on the line. Uh huh. Yep. Sounds reasonable. Thanks for calling.)

Okay, so Michael Lahr, communications director for Rep. Hostettler, confirmed that the gun was loaded, but, he pointed out, there was no bullet in the chamber.

Whew! I just knew there was nothing to the story. Just another congressman "taking care of business" in a scary world.. ∎

Don't Try This at Home

The wise man built his house upon the rock.
The foolish man built his house upon the sand.
Then the foolish man sold his house to me,
so he wasn't so foolish after all, was he?
—from New Testament scripture, or maybe it's from
an old camp song. I forget.

W hich is why, after waking up each morning with the ceiling a little closer to our faces, we're having to spend LOTS of money putting a new foundation under our house. As you know, the way it's supposed to work is first you build your foundation, then you put the house on top of it. Doing it the other way makes absolutely no sense, unless you're tired of listening to the creaks and groans of timbers that make me think I should be walking around with an eye patch, a peg leg, and a parrot on my shoulder. (Actually, the parrot I got already. And my co-workers always know when he's been on my shoulder. CO-WORKER: "Eeeuuu!")

I don't mean to burden you with my personal problems, since you have enough of your own figuring out what those minus signs mean in your 401k statements. Not to mention the sub-prime mortgage scandal that has tarnished just about everyone but the Bush administration which, fortunately, was out of town when it all happened. But don't worry, Congress is on top of this mess, and we can all sleep easier at night knowing that, despite the sickening way elected officials are beholden to corporate interests, integrity in government will be restored. Unless they find a way around it.

But back to my house. The jackhammers start at 7:30, shortly after the morning sun is blotted out by enormous pickup trucks the workers drive. Each is the size of a small ocean liner, with a tool box larger than my refrigerator. Not to be outdone, I bought a tool belt, which I proudly wear when I'm helping the men with the heavy tasks, such as getting them coffee and then collecting the cups afterwards. I'd do a lot more, of course, but I got a splinter early on and they told me with an injury like that I'd better avoid the work area altogether. (They said this between manly giggles, so I knew they were relieved I wasn't more seriously injured.)

I take a certain comfort in having large, silent men around the home, since it's about time the women in my family experience such a phenomenon. My children have grown up assuming that the average American male walks around the house all day in his pajamas, mumbling bitterly about "Johnny Angel" being the last great rock-and-roll song; the kind of man who only puts on work gloves when he changes a light bulb. ("Everyone stand back! I think it's loosening!")

Turns out, My home was built before the invention of right angles, and sadly I never met the crooked little man who used to live here. But on the bright side, there is a certain symmetry in the repair costs being the same as the original price of the home. Unfortunately, prospective buyers might not be impressed by the new foundation wall in the basement—"It's gray and it's GORGEOUS! We can store our decorative wheel barrows down here!" More than likely they'll just complain about there being only one bathroom, which includes a toilet paper holder hanging at a jaunty, cock-eyed angle. (I installed it myself.)

Our house was built around the beginning of the 20th century, before the concept of "workmanship" was in active use in the construction industry. It was built without a basement, presumabley because, since it was such a crappy house to begin with, who'd want to spend any time *underneath* it? Nor did it originally have an indoor bathroom, an amenity that did not become necessary until peeing on trees in the backyard lost its popularity. (Although, sharing a single bathroom with three females has prompted me to single-handedly bring the practice back into fashion.)

We tried to get the insurance company to pay for the repairs, since, as I helpfully theorized, the problems were caused by underground nuclear testing in the 1950s. My agent didn't buy it, but he did offer one of those manly giggles I'm hearing a lot of these days. On the other hand, he reassured us that in the event of a catastrophic fire we'd be fully covered. (But that would be just awful, since then they'd build us a brand new house and who'd want that to happen!?)

As I think about it, I've got two choices:

- I could accidentally pour gasoline over the house and then accidentally set it on fire, right after I had first accidentally removed all the family photo albums, all my guitars, and none of the ceramic roosters that other people in my house are so fond of.

- *Or I could just pay the big, quiet men and keep out of the way. Which is a lot harder than you think, what with all the neat tools around that are heavier and bigger than the Lego versions I'm more familiar with. "Hey guys, could I have a turn at the jackhammer-er-er-er-er-er-er-er-er...oops...was that a gas line?" ■

Mending the Waters

July, 2004

(Editor's Note. The following was written before the mid-term elections of 2004, when gay marriage was expected to once again be a major Republican tactic to get its people to the polls. GOP experts have since simplified this strategy, now that it is understood that gay marriage is a gateway behavior that leads directly to teaching evolution in schools, which is a little too complicated for the average voter. For the foreseeable future, the Republican Party will stick with a more basic message: Vote for the white people.

Having recently been diagnosed with a rare and troubling medical condition—late-onset maturity—it has become unavoidable that I begin to take the world and its woes more seriously.

The coming election, the war, and the painful issues that are dividing our nation are no longer things that I can ignore by simply crawling under my desk, despite the fact that, in doing so, I found my guitar capo. (I had dropped it recently while playing a Neil Diamond song for the pleasure of colleagues passing in the hall, even though none of them stopped to listen. One of the sad ironies of middle age is that, after I finally learned how to play the hits of the '60s, nobody wants me to.)

Don't get me wrong. I am not one to shun controversy. I

have always been a passionate observer of life, but mainly by peeking from behind the door of the janitor's closet down the hall. Now that the world calls out to me—and a court order says I can't peek out at people from the janitor's closet anymore—it's time for me to enter the fray.

This will not be an easy task for me. Take the war, for example, a controversy that has caused a chasm not seen in this country since Charlton Heston dressed up as Moses and commanded the waters to part. (Actually, at the time he was commanding a neutral blue background to part. Technicians added the real water later, when Mr. Heston was safely out of the studio.) Much of the nation is against the war, and the rest—which is to say, mainly Florida, which gets to vote twice, I think—is for it. What is needed—and this is where I come in—is a voice of reason in this tempest of division. In the crucible of public debate, I will be the pestle. Or maybe it's the mortar. Whatever.

FORTUNATELY, others have already tried to resolve these conflicts and bring our nation together. Our political leaders have courageously called Americans to join and fight our common enemy, which, apparently, is gay marriage.

And who can blame them? Without question, the sanctity of marriage is central to our way of life. In fact, we like it so much that many American couples—about half—want to do it again. With somebody else. This 50 percent failure rate is a number we've all grown comfortable with (it's an easy fraction to remember). So do we really want an entirely new demographic group to come in and mess that up, and maybe do it better than the rest of us?

Frankly, I don't much like the sound of "Bobby has two dads." I much prefer the more traditional "Bobby has a mommy and a daddy, whom he sees every other weekend, depending on whether daddy's new girlfriend is in town."

See, it's that kind of reasoning that's most helpful during these difficult times.

And I get that from an experience as a young teenager when my church struggled with a controversy of its own. Back in the late 1960s, members of our Southern Baptist congregation had grown complacent in their faith. There was an evil in our midst, and that evil was, you guessed it...slacks.

That's right, slacks. But thanks to our pastor, a man ever-watchful for the temptations of the flesh (as well as for choir members who tried to park in his space on Sundays), we stopped Satan and left him quaking in his boots. Or possibly his flip-flops.

It was during Vacation Bible School in the heat of an Indiana summer. Some of the teachers—women who selfishly worked for God's favor by spending their mornings teaching little kids about Jesus—started wearing slacks. They had already tried to wear shorts because of the heat, but the pastor was quick to point out that the heat of Hell was much hotter, so they'd better wear dresses like the Bible says (or would have, if God hadn't forgotten to put it in).

The pastor's ultimatum was questioned by some church members, specifically the women's husbands who were themselves unable to help out in Bible school because they had to work downtown in air conditioning. They reminded him that these were fine Christian women who should be trusted to know what best to wear. The pastor responded by saying, prayerfully, "Not as long as I'm pastor of this church." Which gave the husbands an idea. For the betterment of the kingdom, the pastor soon resumed his successful house-painting career. (I won't even mention that the next pastor preached against the sin of pantsuits, because that would weaken an otherwise inspirational story.)

I'll never forget how that controversy was settled in my old church. It is a reminder of what lay leaders—particularly husbands who appreciate home-cooked meals—can do in a time of crisis. I'm grateful that I was a part of it, at least the part I could see from inside the janitor's closet. ∎

Jury Duty Calls,
Or You Can Go to Prison

Jury duty is one of those responsibilities of citizenship that reminds us that the American justice system is the best in the world. It also reminds us that, if at all possible, we never want to have anything to do with the American justice system. Not ever.

If you're not a law-abiding citizen when you first report for jury duty, by the end of the day you definitely are. You never want to go back there again, in *any* capacity. It's like prison, only without the exercise yard. By the end of my two days I was scratching a crude calendar into the back of the seat in front of me. I wanted to speak to an attorney. I wanted my rights read to me. I wanted to yell "GUARD!!" but that would have interrupted the catatonia of the other 200 people trapped in a room with no windows and 12 ceiling-mounted TVs.

As we waited to be called to trial, we were apparently being tested by having to watch something called *Regis and Kathie Lee.* I have heard of this program. I have also heard that there are people who watch this of their own free will. But here in this large room there was no choice, no escaping this Regis and Kathie Lee person (or perhaps it was two separate people).

"Come on Steve. Take your shirt off. Let's see the kind of hunk that stars on General Hospital!" [frenzied screams from

audience]

I glance up. Maybe the people in the TV audience are themselves waiting for a jury assignment, except they're in a more creative city that teaches pity and compassion to its jurors by making them watch celebrities.

But my mind was becoming numb from the noise. Those around me had already lost their will to resist. They slouched, unmoving, staring up at the televisions with heavy lids and blank expressions, newspapers slowly sliding out of their lifeless fingers and gathered in loose piles on the floor.

They were the undead.

I had to get out of there. I moved quickly toward a distant door labeled "Smoker's Room" figuring a cancer risk is better than insanity.

"Today we're going to be talking about 'What Turns You On!'" the television calls after me as I desperately pulled open the door. A quantity of smoke that could only come from an oil tanker explosion began stinging my face and lungs as I stepped into the room. Two dozen people sat in silence as smoke poured from their faces, their hands, their clothing, and not one of them was lunging for a fire extinguisher.

They looked up angrily at the intruder who stood at the door, permitting unwelcome fresh air into the room. I shuddered at the sight and made my way back to the ever-smiling receptionist. May I go downstairs for some air, perhaps some coffee? "I'm sorry, sir. No one is allowed to leave once you've checked in."

Defeated, I walked slowly back to The Place of Great Noise. *"The Women of the KKK...today on* Oprah!*"*

If Dr. Kevorkian had walked into that room and asked for volunteers, he could have filled a good-sized bus.

Attempting some reassurance, the receptionist called after me, "The judge said he'd call for his first panel around 9." (It was 10:30.) "Just go back to your seat, and make yourself at home." Yes, I thought to myself, I could make myself a home, if I had right tools. I certainly had enough time.

Finally, my number is called and things happened quickly. In the time it takes to shout "Guilty!" we are seated in Courtroom Number 5.

IT IS COLD HERE. Very cold. Is this to keep us awake, or to keep those dying of boredom from decomposing too quickly?

Interestingly, I'm seated next to Sander Vanocur, the former TV news correspondent whom I remember watching in my pajamas when I was a kid. I don't mention this to him (the part about the pajamas), but I attempt to start a conversation by offering him a Lifesaver. He declines. But, who could blame him? It was a yellow one, and I would have got the red one just below that. This guy's no dummy.

"All rise." Actually, with the pent-up tension I carried from the other room I would have preferred "All bend down and touch your toes." The judge walks in, and a uniformed man reads the oath of service, to which we reply in unison, "I Will." "I Do." "Yes." "Could you repeat the question? You see, I've been trapped in a large room with more TVs than Circuit City and...."

"If any of you have ever been a victim of a crime, or convicted of a crime, please approach the bench."

Yes! Finally. El Rejecto! That's what always gets me excused: Because I'm both. I've been robbed at gunpoint and I've been convicted of crimes of conscience. Ironically, I was not sent to a special jail for people of conscience. Rather, I was sent to the jail for people who rob at gunpoint, which was very uncomfortable for a guy who might as well be wearing a sign that says "Hi. I'm new here!" Though, in truth, I nearly killed a guy in prison. When he asked how long I was in for I told him "10 weekends in jail for a protest." "Weekends! WEEKENDS?!" he roared, falling to the floor clutching his chest in laughter, struggling to catch his breath. Apparently he had not been offered this particular option. Like I said, I almost killed the guy.

So anyway, nobody wants me on a jury: too prejudiced in both directions, they figure. Plus, I don't know what "approach the bench" means. Do you go right up to it, or just sort of lean toward it? Are you allowed to reach up and feel the smooth wood grain or will the judge hit you with that little hammer thingy?

Anyway, for the third time in as many years I'm sent back to Planet Television to finish my sentence, against which there can be no protest, no defense, no appeal.

Objection overruled. ■

It's Almost Over...

September, 2004

This has been a tough election season, a grueling, no-holds-barred slugfest filled with rumors, lies, and innuendo. And that was just on Fox News.

Thankfully, it's almost time to move beyond the bickering and divisiveness and start thinking about life after Nov. 2. But first, Karl Rove...YOU'RE A STINKER! Okay, now we can move beyond the bickering and divisiveness.

Depending on who is elected, we could see a very different future for this country. If one candidate wins, our nation will roll up its sleeves and begin the arduous task of recovering from a debilitating deficit, an unprecedented rollback of environmental protection, and an ill-conceived war.

Come to think of it, that sounds like a lot of work. So forget that.

If the other candidate wins, the to-do list will be much shorter: Move to Canada.

Regardless of the results, there is no question it will be another victory for the democratic electoral process which, since our nation's very first presidential election, has always represented the will of the people. Except for the last time.

But no matter. The process works, and once again throughout the land freedom will be ringing. (Or maybe that's just the sound of seniors counting their change at the pharmacy, seeing if they have enough for the rest of the month.)

Perhaps more important, this election again confirmed that the rights of the minority—a core principle of our democracy—are still being protected with vigor. In establishing a government of majority rule, our founding fathers understood that protections must also exist for those outside the mainstream, such as themselves, and that people should never be discriminated against because of their economic position, such as theirs, since they were rich and most everybody else was poor. (Back then you could tell the difference by the powdered wigs, which rich people don't wear today. They'd like to, but it's hard to hold on to a powdered wig when you're rushing to the bank with another tax rebate check.)

WE HAVE TO admit we'll miss some things about this election season. We'll miss Vice President Richard "Dick" Cheney warning Americans that the sky was falling and that, if you voted for John Kerry, a meteor could hit your house at any moment. Cheney later clarified that, in all probability, a meteor would just hit somewhere in your neighborhood.

We'll also miss the vice president claiming that stem cell research is a states' rights issue that does not require constitutional protection, after acknowledging that his own daughter is, in fact, a stem cell. (Although I might be getting that mixed up.)

We'll miss John Kerry defending his voting record with fascinating and circuitous explanations—frequently using the English language. Sadly, his heartfelt clarifications were often lost on voters who, despite trying really hard to listen and understand, can be forgiven if their attention wandered. ("Oh look. A butterfly!")

We'll miss our image of Karl Rove—trembling with glee,

lips moist with anticipation—as he guided the Bush campaign toward another detour from the real issues, forcing the Democrats to vigorously deny that their candidate was ever married to Jane Fonda.

To be fair, we have to feel sorry for Rove, who was unable to capitalize on a study released late in the campaign that people with Alzheimer's disease actually vote more than healthy people. True fact: In the 2000 election, an elderly man in Florida wanted to vote for Franklin Roosevelt, so his wife entered the voting booth with him and filled out his ballot. It is unclear if the results of the election ushered in the New Deal he was hoping for, but what is clear is that his wife voted twice. In Florida.

Sigh.

We'll miss former Vice President Al "Al" Gore getting emotional during his speeches. In a stark departure from his earlier campaign (slogan: "I'm Alive. No, Really."), he often spewed invective against White House policies. Fortunately, people in the front row had been warned and were dressed appropriately. (When former vice presidents spew, they've got range, and that invective stuff doesn't wash out.)

Looking a little farther back, we'll particularly miss the heated discussions over the president's faith-based initiative, a good idea that was abandoned because it was impossible to pronounce without a lisp. OFFICIAL: "This faith-bathed...no, I mean faste-based...er, fashed-bashed.... Forget it. Just give the money to the Pentagon." ∎

Driving Miss Crazy

There comes a time in every man's life when he has to begin a sentence with a really bad cliché. This is one of those times. You see, words are not coming easy to me these days. And when I do speak, I seem to be talking in gibberish, running my words together in a strange new dialect: "YOU'REGOINGTOOFAST!" I'll say, seemingly at random. Or "STAYINYOUROWNLANE..."WATCH THECURB!"

And I'm talking louder than I used to, as if I were trying to alert someone far away. An ambulance, perhaps.

It's just a coincidence, of course, that this only happens when I'm in a car being driven by my oldest daughter, the first to reach the milestone of obtaining a learner's permit. By law, she cannot operate the vehicle alone. For the safety of others on the road, she is required to have a frightened and babbling adult in the car with her. And since I say things like "LOOK OUT!" with less emotion than my wife, the family has chosen me for this task. (Our thoughtful 14-year-old generously offered to take my place, so that we parents could "just relax at home," but we declined.)

And so we drive, every day, through the nation's capital, negotiating its mean streets, avoiding potholes and drunken diplomats (both of which are immune from prosecution), and, above all, trying to minimize the number of pedestrians we knock over in the crosswalks.

HAVING SPENT the past decade driving these two youngsters to school every day, the question for me is, NOW what am I supposed to do? When I was driving I was very busy, what with turning down the radio, jotting down notes for the day ahead, shaving, and occasionally trimming my toenails on the dashboard. But now I just have to sit there and cringe. Or mess with stuff on the door. "DAD! STOP PLAYING WITH THE DOORLOCKS. IT'S NOT GOOD FOR THE MECHANISM!" Okay, so I can't do that anymore. Maybe I could get one of those Fisher-Price steering wheels (with its own horn!).

In fairness to her, our young driver has just about mastered the basics of driving (except for the part where you're supposed to slow down when pulling over to the curb. And, of course, parallel parking. "Why couldn't a helicopter just lower us down into the parking space? Is that too much to ask?!"). So I'm almost ready to begin teaching her the more subtle nuances of urban driving, such as:

- Optional stop signs. Busy drivers are well-advised to take advantage of these traffic aids, particularly when they're running late.

- Directional honking; also known as "vehicle-specific" honking. When you're a few cars back and the lead driver fails to notice the light has turned green, it's your job to get his or her attention without disturbing the cars immediately in front of you. New drivers especially need to learn this technique, since it avoids misunderstandings that occur when the guy in front of you starts waving a pistol.

- Sometimes it's a bad idea to try to outrun police cars that are chasing you. It's a judgment call, of course, but often it's best just to pull over.

- Speed limits are for comparison purposes only. How often have you asked yourself this question: "Is George W. Bush the first president who had a C average in college?" If so, then obviously you haven't been paying attention. But this often happens on a highway at night when the speed limit signs appear right when you're trying to close your eyes for a couple miles to keep from falling asleep. Actually the best time to look at a speed sign is when you wake up with your car in a ditch. Then you can simply walk over to the sign and read it up close, carefully writing down what it says before calling the tow truck.

- Be real nice to your insurance agent. That way, he'll be equally nice to you when you explain that the six-car pileup you caused wasn't your fault at all. In fact, you didn't even see it happen since, at the time, you were busy trying to find some gum in the glove compartment.

ADMITTEDLY, there is a limit to what a child can learn from her father, so we will soon pass her on to a professional instructor to teach her the finer points of driving, just as soon as he learns English. And since children respond much better when taught outside the home, I plan to give the instructor a list of other things to teach. Including:

- How to put in a new roll of toilet paper (no one in my houses has ever done this except me).

- How to change the cat litter (see above), and why this is SO important in the summer months.

Spending time with an instructor also reduces the insurance premiums for the new driver. Other ways to reduce premiums include making good grades, being nice to your parents, and promising not to date until college. (Okay. So I made up the first one.) Our insurance agent also promised discounts if we whisper "Don't crash" 10 times every night into our sleeping daughter's ear. Which is no problem, since we already whisper "Don't smoke" to our other sleeping daughter. And so far that seems to be working. (At least it's working for everybody else in her room, except for the cockatiel, who's got yellow stains on his beak and this odd hacking cough.) ■

Decision 2004

I 've always wanted my own lawyer. Even though I've come this far without one, I still envy people who, with obvious satisfaction, can say, "I'll see what my lawyer thinks about that." Having a lawyer elevates one's status in life and suggests a higher level of security than you get with, say, your own plumber, which I do have.

But it's not the same. Granted, no one would argue that a plumber is, in almost every way, far more useful than a lawyer. But invoking his name after a minor car accident doesn't quite carry the authority desired. "You think this was MY fault?! Well, you'll be hearing from my plumber about this!"

Coincidentally, my office doesn't have a plumber, but it does have a lawyer. Nice guy, I'm told, although I've never seen him around the office. And if I did see him, presumably he would not be wearing a heavy tool belt that made his workpants ride low on his hips, exposing more information than necessary while bending down to repair a leaky legal brief, or whatever it is that lawyers do.

Lately our lawyer has been giving us a lot of advice about what nonprofit organizations can and cannot publish during an election year. Sojourners is a 501(c)(3), a federal nonprofit designation which, as I recall, was also the name of that robot in

Star Wars. But then Star Wars is a copyright-protected motion picture that our lawyer advises we shouldn't even mention. (In that movie the robot also had an intimate friendship with a little robot called R2D2. Not that there's anything wrong with that. And we imply nothing about their relationship, which, according to our lawyer, is also none of our business.)

Obviously, our lawyer is a cautious man. While he understands Sojourners' calling to speak the truth to power, he doesn't see why we have to do it out in public, as opposed to, say, inside a windowless room someplace. "Just talk amongst yourselves," our attorney suggests, "preferably using telepathy, so that nobody actually hears you and gets offended." In other words, don't bother people with your prophetic opinions, he tells us, especially innocent people minding their own business, such as politicians, or the federal government.

TO WHICH I reply "pshaw," maybe even a stronger "feh!" Sojourners will not be silenced. Not by governments, political extremists, or attorneys on retainer. (I had a retainer once... never mind.) We will not hide our light under a bushel (no!), or confine our powerful words of truth to a small room. Unless there'll be snacks.

But snacks aside, the mission of Sojourners has always been to preach the gospel of peace and reconciliation to a troubled world. We do this from a deep sense of calling, and also because, let's face it, Spiderman can't do it alone.

Unfortunately, the first rule of nonprofits—take no partisan political positions—has been difficult in this critical election year. (The second rule—make no profit—we're already good at.) This is probably the most important vote of our lives and, despite our lawyer's risk-aversion, a clear moral voice is needed. And since "moral" is our middle name (actually, it was "Beatrice," but we changed it), we feel we have no choice but to endorse a candidate. Our nation is desperate for a positive outcome of this election, even if neither candidate is a plumber and, as a consequence, not particularly useful.

AND SPEAKING of lawyers, let's look at the two candidates (Ralph Nader, put your hand down). John Kerry is the Democratic nominee and he is running an aggressive campaign to bring a just end to the Vietnam War. Never mind that it's been over for a while, he's focused.

George Bush, the Republican nominee, is currently the president, and he may have been a little unprepared for his own war, as revealed in this recent White House meeting with Secretary of Defense Donald Rumsfeld:

RUMSFELD: We've got more trouble in Iraq.

BUSH: Where?

RUMSFELD: Najaf.

BUSH: Gesundheit.

To us the choice is clear. Only one man can lead our nation into a dangerous and uncertain future, a future that may be filled with actions of shocking unpredictability, such as Dick Cheney helping an old person across the street. It's time for me to endorse the best candidate for the job, and that man is (Editor's Note: SUPPORT OUR TROOPS!) ∎

Last One in the Gene Pool...

Belated congratulations to scientists working on the human genome project, who have discovered that humans are more highly developed than roundworms. (Scientists in the same project also feel humans are genetically superior to a mustard plant, although this has yet to be confirmed.)

The reason for the comparison is that humans have roughly the same number of genes as the roundworm, although ours produce more proteins and work harder, human teenagers being the one exception. (This may explain why teen-agers at the time of the study listened to the Backstreet Boys, one of the so-called "boy bands" who, ironically, sound like girls. Admittedly, my generation also listened to boy bands, and when Frankie Valli sang "Walk Like a Man" in his trademark falsetto it sounded more like "Walk Like a Man Just Hit by an Underthrown Fastball."

(But I digress.)

Now, it's no surprise to me that humans are smarter than roundworms (*losers!*), and, although there are a couple of people at the office who have much in common with mustard plants, I think this is pretty good evolutionary news. In fact, I feel vindicated in my childhood hopes that the roundworm toughs at my high school would one day regret the unkind things they said to me. (I prayed they'd have to eat their words—although, as it turns out, they don't so much eat them as secrete an enzyme that is then re-absorbed through their outer membranes.)

Not surprising, roundworms took the news hard and complained that this was just another in a long series of indignities they have endured throughout history. Bad enough that Jesus chose the mustard seed for an important analogy—they always felt "the Kingdom of God is like a roundworm" had a much better ring to it—but this latest slight was a little hard to swallow (although, again, if you're paying attention, they don't actually swallow).

Before this scientific revelation returned them to their original biological status (parasitica mos flushworthi), roundworms had grown accustomed to being treated as genetic equals to humans. They had no qualms about demanding the same respect at fine restaurants and clothiers, or jauntily riding down the highway with the top down and the wind blowing—James Dean-like—through their microscopic follicles. But people were wearying of the "annoying little parasites" and the way the tabloids obsessively reported their every move. ("ROUNDWORM BEHIND JENNIFER AND BRAD SPLIT".... "SHED 10 POUNDS IN ONE DAY WITH CELEBRITY ROUNDWORM DIET!")

Many felt it was time for the roundworm to reassume its proper genetic place, alongside other simple organisms such as the sea cucumber and former Rep. Tom DeLay (who has yet to end the speculation that he is, genetically speaking, more closely linked to ultra-conservative ocean plankton).

THE HUMAN GENOME project examines one of the last great mysteries of life, and scientists feel that, once fully understood, there will be only a few remaining secrets to explore. These include: subatomic particles (or, in scientific shorthand, "Bill

O'Reilly"), the basic structure of light, and the complex question of how to fold women's underwear. (Are you supposed to end up with a triangle or a parallelogram?) And, more important, why I have to do it in the first place.

In other science-related news, Kansas' newly elected school board voted to once again to ban teaching evolution in schools. The nearly unanimous vote came shortly after it was discovered that the previous school board had evolved from roundworms.

And speaking of evolution, we were pleased to see that, throughout his presidency, George Bush has bravely rejected the draconian rules of proper pronunciation that have, over the millennia, come to inhibit our language. For instance, his repeated use of "nucular"—when the arcane strictures of English require the word "nuclear" to be correctly spoken and spelled—was a clear sign that the shackles of grammatical propriety need no longer chafe nor constrict our society. Clearly, this is welcome leadership from a president who does not "Quayle" in the presence of those who purport to speak good grammar. He's has been a higher calling. ∎

Shouldn't They Call It
the "Really Deep Canyon"?

Helllloooooooooo!" That's what I shouted over the Grand Canyon when we first pulled up in the car during our cross-country trip. You're supposed to do that. Whenever you see a great big hole placed inconveniently between you and your destination, you have to get out of your car and embarrass your family by yelling loudly. For maximum effect, there should be a lot of strangers around, ensuring that your teen-age daughter will never speak to you again "for as long as I live!" or until you get back into the car, whichever comes first. "If you EVER do something like that again, Dad..."

I'm hearing this a lot lately, now that I've apparently entered a period of my life where I routinely do things outside the narrow range of teen-age acceptability, such as innocently walking through the house in my pajamas—my OWN house, mind you—when she has friends over. Was that so wrong? I think I look *good* in matching plaid tops and bottoms, accessorized with comfortable suede slippers. (And what party doesn't need a touch of plaid to perk things up?)

But back to the Grand Canyon, a geological phenomenon that really gets in the way of people trying to make Vegas by dinner time ("What the...! [sound of car brakes squealing] How did THIS get here?! What, they couldn't have dug it off to the SIDE of the interstate?!!")

Much of our trip from Washington D.C. was narrated by our 11-year-old who told us of all the wonders of the Grand Canyon, giving particular emphasis to the famous mule ride down to the bottom. She couldn't wait for our whole family to do this.

But I know the dirty little secret about that ride. A friend used to spend her summers selling tickets for the popular mule trip. Popular, that is, at the beginning. Decidedly *un*-popular about five minutes later when the tourist realizes he has just paid $200 to sit on an animal who walks right on the very edge of a narrow trail, presumably to listen to loose stones scrabbling down the mile-deep drop-off. Of course, the noise of those falling stones is obscured by the sad, pitiful human noises, punctuated by short screams of terror. Hearing her recount this from the relative safety of our office building a few years ago, I immediately updated my personal creed of beliefs to include "not riding a mule into the Grand Canyon." (This replaces "Don't tug on Superman's cape," since someone finally convinced me that he's just a mythical superhero. Oh well. There's still Batman.)

So we didn't do the mule ride, which was disappointing to our youngest, but I quickly pointed out that disappointment is one of those emotions that living people have, as opposed to the complete lack of emotions experienced by deceased mule riders.

We could have hiked down into the canyon instead, except for the signs that said "Don't hike down into the canyon." It seems that people forget that hiking the full mile down to the bottom means, once there, they'll probably look up and say "Hey, like, we have to hike all the way back up now. By the way, is it just me or is it really hot down here?" Yes, it gets as high as 115 degrees at the bottom in the daytime, but don't worry, at night it gets down to just above freezing. A hiking wonderland? You bet.

To make up for not risking our lives in the Grand Canyon, we considered caving, which also poses a high degree of danger since the snack bar inside nearby Carlsbad Caverns supposedly has the *worst* hot dogs. (Parenthetical note to cavers: Lights on the ceiling, wooden walkways on the floor, snack bar...now THAT'S caving!)

THE AMERICAN WEST is truly an awesome place, with skies that stretch from horizon to horizon (unlike the American East, where the horizon stretches from liquor store to liquor store.) The West is big, with big skies, big canyons, and big shoulders (oops, that's Chicago). The West is so big they say things like, "Yeah I know where that is. You go up this here road about 430 miles and turn left. Then you're halfway there."

The high point of our trip was the week we spent in a mountain cabin, right next to a spring-fed stream. There is no better rest than sleeping next to a quietly gurgling stream, except for when you get up several times a night and groggily stumble into the bathroom to shake the toilet handle. "Oh yeah," you remember, "...gurgling stream."

Unfortunately, our enthusiasm for the cabin was diminished somewhat when a neighbor walked over and reported he had seen "more bears this year than ever before," to which I replied, in the timeless words of my mountain-taming ancestors, "Monopoly, anyone!?" I quickly began planning a week's worth of great indoor fun, telling the kids "a cabin can be a wonderfully cozy place...DON'T OPEN THAT DOOR!...a place you never really have to leave, okay?" The neighbor assured us there is nothing to fear from bears as long as you don't run when you see one. "Just yell real loud, or give a sharp whistle, and they'll go away." He forgot that in this particular circumstance, a person's whistle may lack the required sharpness, sounding more like "PPHLIPSTH!" or "TWEEPFTH!"

The neighbor guy (who was beginning to really get on my nerves) also mentioned casually that we probably shouldn't cook any bacon, even indoors, since bears are etremely attracted to the odor. I'm certain this is all good advice, but if I were to actually see a bear close by I'd probably forget to whistle, and run away as fast as possible. I would also probably scream loudly the first thing that came into my mind: "BACON! I GOT YOUR BACON HERE! WHO WANTS BACON?!"

But otherwise the mountain was beautiful. At least the parts we could see through the window. ∎

Lab-Tested and Ready

January, 2005

Now that a chastened George W. Bush has packed his bags and returned to his first love—brush-clearing—our government can at last face the nation's challenges with a reasonable hope of success.

Oops. Sorry. I wrote that paragraph a while ago and forgot to change it. What I meant to say is, now that an *un-chastened* George W. Bush has been reinstalled in the White House he can finally ask the question that is permitted only to a second-term president who has earned the respect of the nation and the trust of the military: Namely, where do they keep the aliens?

You know, the bodies of unlucky beings from other planets who, because of a spacecraft malfunction, were forced to land on an unfriendly planet inhabited by petulant primitives with little tolerance for life outside their own narrow world of experience.

But enough about Jerry Falwell.

Let's talk about science, and not the kind the Bush administration rolls its eyes at and routinely says "BORING!" whenever something like global warming is mentioned. (Not that our nation's leaders are ignorant of environmental issues, but I heard that House Speaker Dennis Hastert thinks "hubris" is one of those new hybrid cars.)

No, we're talking about REAL science, important science, the kind of science that has created...homosexual rats. (And you thought this writer is never serious.)

Scientists have discovered that the so-called "gay gene"— also known as the "not-that-there's-anything-wrong-with-that gene"—results in a smaller hypothalamus in rats, and therefore, scientists have concluded (by jumping), also human males. (I'm already bracing for the coming flood of e-mails titled "Enlarge Your Hypothalamus!") This condition can be replicated in experiments with laboratory rats that cause them to exhibit overtly homosexual behavior.

That's pretty much where I stopped reading, however, because let's face it, rats are ooky enough without having to imagine their dating habits. Unless, of course, the behavior observed was rats tidying up their cages, taking extra time grooming, or sending thoughtful notes to scientists on their birthday. But that would be perpetuating stereotypes, and if there's anything I can't stand it's perpetuating stereotypes about rodents, such as the fact that Tom DeLay hoards food pellets.

Scientists experiment more on rats than on any other animal, and it's not just because they lack union representation. (Actually, as a class, laboratory rats have better benefits than Wal-Mart employees.) Rats are used because they contain a similar genetic code to humans. When pressed, researchers will admit the one major difference between the two species is when a human scurries across the street at night nobody involuntarily shudders "Eeeeeeeeuuu!!!" and then throws a garbage can at him. Other than that, however, rats and humans are pretty much alike. Which is why concern is often raised when studies discover substances that cause cancer in rats.

To be honest, rats getting cancer has never really bothered me. In fact—and I hope this doesn't seem cruel—I'm all for rats getting cancer. Or, for that matter, tuberculosis. While we're at it, throw in irritable bowel syndrome and a root canal. The point is, we have enough of those slimy little guys running around already, and not just at the National Rifle Association. The less rats, the better, has always been my motto. Well, that, and "follow every rainbow."

On the other hand, scientists working for the U.S. tobacco industry have discovered that rats who smoke look really cool.)

RECENTLY, RESEARCHERS have also begun experimenting with pigs, in some cases successfully implanting human tissue. In the near future, entire organs could be harvested from livestock, an advancement that would greatly benefit those currently waiting for life-saving transplants, such as Donald Trump, who's in line for a soul.

Despite the obvious medical benefits of this research, however, not all would welcome such advances. Take the Tin Man, for instance: "I don't have to give you a heart," said the kindly wizard, his warm smile calming the fears of Dorothy and her friends. "It was here all along. In that pig over there."

Others would fully embrace the benefits. If such a procedure had been available years ago, the Kennedy family wouldn't have needed an Austrian body builder to improve its gene pool. And it's pretty much assumed that the current governor of California, in his early years, would not have hesitated in adding, say, pig transplants to his admirable model of healthy living, which includes exercise, sensible eating, and massive injections of steroids. ∎

Finally, Fiscal Responsibility

(Editor's note: Some of the following observations may sound a little mean now, such as the churlish reference to a major defense contractor expecting more than its fair share of the nation's annual budget. On reflection, this may have been too harsh. After all, when President Eisenhower warned against the growing power of the "military industrial complex" he was merely raising a rhetorical question, right?)

Despite Congressional recalcitrance—which most doctors say comes from not having enough fiber in the diet—the White House is showing courageous leadership around the issues of fiscal sustainability, in particular the future of critical entitlement programs such as Social Security, Medicare, and Lockheed Martin.

The good news is that, in its recently released 2006 budget proposal, the White House has finally confronted powerful lobbies and special interests and is calling for cuts in government programs that have for decades placed an enormous burden on our national treasury. With apologies to no one, the Bush budget simply pulls the plug on these special interests and their narrow agendas.

Such as schools for American Indian children.

Also, emergency food aid for the poor.

These are just two of the wasteful programs against which

the Bush administration has vowed to stand up and say, simply, "Enough." In its bold commitment to cut the federal deficit, the president has vowed to bring an end to the unchecked influence wielded by the undernourished and the undereducated who, since World War II, have been gorging themselves at the public trough. Meanwhile, lobbyists for underrepresented groups—such as the defense industry—have been forced to grovel for the crumbs left over.

If this budget passes, gone will be the days when lawmakers cringe at the sight of the poor and the elderly walking the halls of government like they own the place. No more will minorities "have their way" with legislators who are forced to take meetings—frequently precluding their previously-scheduled time with patriotic representatives of the oil industry—to listen to these groups place their own selfish needs above the good of the country.

No more will legislators cower before bullying students pressing their demands for more college aid. From now on those annoying students will have to pay their own way, and write the check themselves, just like the parents of rich kids do.

And no more will assistance to the physically disadvantaged be the third rail of American politics. It's bad enough that, because of draconian accessibility laws, the handicapped can simply roll their one-sided agendas into congressional offices, while offshore-drilling lobbyists are forced to take the stairs.

THIS RIGHTEOUS OUTRAGE was partly triggered when White House officials noticed that new school construction on American Indian reservations comprised almost .00000000000003 percent of the federal budget. Clearly, the time for compromise was over.

Not to say that American Indian children don't have as much right to federal funds as, say, a worthy corporate citizen like Halliburton. But American Indians are still peeved about being moved—completely at government expense, I might add—to their spacious lands, despite the fact that, should a market develop for sun-baked rock and cactus, they are sitting on a potential goldmine. Which begs the question: Where is the gratitude?

Understandably, the White House proposal assumes that tax breaks for the wealthy will be extended in perpetuity—a Latin expression that means, literally, "If I didn't need all this money, Granmere wouldn't have left it for me in the first place." And the administration fully expected criticism for this and other efforts to repeal the New Deal. Although White House officials concede that the name they came up with—the Raw Deal—has not tested well with focus groups, the president is undeterred. In his view, the needs of the poor and the sick have for too long dominated the national agenda. He wants the American people to know that, finally, there is someone in the Oval Office who understands that the wealthy are people, too.

After all, the back seat of a limousine can be a very lonely place. ∎

Quiet on the Set

Film stardom is an elusive dream for most, including even yours truly, whom many have credited with talents well-suited for the big screen. My home town is still talking about my performance as the "voice from offstage" in one of our high school plays. (The words "Delivery, ma'am!" have, if I may say so, never been spoken with so much emotional authority.) So it was not a complete surprise to me recently when I was singled out by a major Hollywood director during the making of a major Hollywood film.

But I'm getting ahead of myself.

BEING THE ONLY person in my house who works near a shopping area, I'm often tasked with purchasing various personal products that the other members of my family can't buy during the day. Almost weekly these women give me a list of products to pick up at the nearby CVS drugstore. Suffice it to say, these are not "manly" items, products that would, in the process of purchasing them, suggest to the cashier my innate masculinity, or convey to other patrons that "here's a gent to be reckoned with." In fact, I'll even admit to some embarrassment at approaching the checkout counter with a basket full of gender-specific personal products, at times feeling the need to grab another items to provide some balance. (The latest copy of Guns 'n Ammo magazine or a bottle of Old Spice usually does the trick.)

I was on such an errand when I literally stepped into the path of stardom (and, quite frankly, was rather rudely asked to get out of the way). Inside the drugstore the cashier had thoughtfully jammed my purchases into a single plastic bag which, stretched tightly over the packages, revealed to just about anybody that I had "confidence, both day and night," on account of the "extra absorbency."

Unable to conceal the purchases under my shirt—I wear a medium-small, so there's not much fabric left for surreptitiousness—I stepped into the street heading back to my office. About halfway across it occurred to me that my usually bustling inner-city neighborhood was quiet, the block practically devoid of cars. I was beginning to wonder about this transformation—Was it a holiday? Had Washington, D.C., finally become a tranquil and civil place to live? Okay, was it a holiday?—when a voice from a loudspeaker called out, "GUY WITH THE CVS BAG!"

It took a second for me to realize I was the subject of this announcement. If someone had shouted, "Guy with the extra absorbency bag!" it would have registered immediately, and I would've whirled around in a powerful display of virile athleticism and shouted back, "IT'S NOT FOR ME! SEE, I LIVE WITH THESE THREE WOMEN AND...."

"Guy with the CVS bag! GET OFF THE STREET!" the amplified voice rang out again. I stopped and looked to my left and saw, a half block away, a man in a director's chair sitting on the centerline of the street. Next to him was a big movie camera pointed directly at me, and next to that was a guy shouting through a bullhorn. Behind him were about 50 people with walkie-talkies and clipboards and they were all looking expectantly at me, as if they wanted something. Something from my CVS bag, perhaps.

It finally occurred to me that I was being filmed, so I immediately began to turn my indecisiveness into *deeply dramatic* indecisiveness, until a large man with a walkie-talkie and clipboard appeared from behind a nearby tree. Apparently under the impression that I could not walk, he dragged me quite forcefully back behind said tree. He seemed in a hurry.

For which I should be grateful, as it turned out, since about five seconds later there appeared, at the very spot where I had been standing, two helicopters flying very fast and very low and very loudly. One of them turned in a tight arc directly above me before it roared away into the sky.

"Oh," I said. And I meant it.

"Cut!" said the bullhorn voice, and then, "Okay people, let's do it again. Don't anybody move."

By "anybody" he apparently meant me. At least the large man with the clipboard thought so, and he pressed my shoulders even more forcefully into the tree. I was beginning to feel like we should be introduced or perhaps plan a lunch together—nothing too formal, of course—when those same two helicopters came whooshing down right next to us again, this time followed along the street by a line of cars which sped a few yards and then intentionally crashed into each other. At which point the bullhorn voice yelled "Cut!" again, and then "Lunch!" and the drivers got out of their cars and left without exchanging insurance information.

My captor relaxed his grip and walked off without so much as a word, not even a poignant backward glance, despite the fact that we had been through so much together. Such is the jaded nature of film-making, I was discovering, where strong personal bonds are formed only to be broken, willy-nilly, without thought for the wounded hearts left behind. Hollywood can be a brutal mistress, even to those of us too wise to be seduced by her charms.

THE FILM IS called Enemy of the State, starring Will Somebody, and from what I could see it breaks new cinematic ground. I don't see many movies so I could be wrong about this, but it seems to me the practice of using automobile crashes and dramatic helicopter chases is very innovative and could set new standards in the film industry. One wonders how much better Breakfast At Tiffany's could have been, for example, had a helicopter dramatically passed overhead during the final scene.

If this film achieves box office success it will derive not only from the drama of helicopters but also from the powerful acting of its cast, not the least of which was a lone thespian whose evocative work off-camera produced, in my opinion, a palpable dramatic effect.

It's just a pity that few—okay, nobody—in my office wants to hear about it. ■

John Bolton, We Never Knew Ye (mercifully)

July, 2005

At press time, the nomination of John Bolton as U.N. ambassador had been put on hold while the U.S. Senate—our most deliberative legislative body—reacted to the shocking photos of Saddam Hussein in his underwear. Male lawmakers were shaken by pictures of a ruthless dictator wearing the same form-fitting briefs that their own mothers had dressed them in shortly after each had passed that first test of manhood: going potty. In response, the Senate passed a resolution that all American men should immediately switch to boxer shorts. The resolution is nonbinding—much like boxer shorts—but carries the full weight of a legislative body that was outraged at the sight of a tyrant known for his brutality wearing undergarments known for their move-as-you-move comfort. "We had to take a stand, even to the point of personal sacrifice," said Senate Majority Leader Bill Frist, shifting his feet awkwardly due to the unaccustomed feel of a garment that, because of a design flaw, tends to bunch up when you walk.

BUT BACK TO THIS Bolton thing (you thought I forgot). You have to feel sorry for President Bush. After all, nominating

John Bolton as U.N. ambassador was just a quick favor for his friend Condoleezza Rice. A loyal and unassuming public servant, Ms. Rice wanted nothing more than to perform her duties with integrity and, if possible, a four-hour train ride away from Mr. Bolton. But making that happen wasn't easy.

It turns out that Bolton has had trouble working well with others in his various government jobs, and was known for throwing tantrums and refusing to go down for his afternoon nap. (And, for the fifth year in a row, he failed to receive the State Department's coveted Mr. Congeniality award.)

Thus, few were surprised when Bolton's nomination was held up by Democrats on the Senate Committee on Foreign Relations who, to the chagrin of the White House, took seriously their constitutional role of annoy and dissent. But Republican senators were also troubled by the lengthy list of complaints against the nominee, which include bullying subordinates, pressuring intelligence analysts, and once screaming at a colleague while chasing her down the hallway of a Russian hotel. (To be fair, your typical diplomatic mission to Moscow provides little in the way of entertainment, aside from chasing colleagues down hallways in the middle of the night. I mean, for cryin' out loud, the hotel didn't even have cable!)

IN THE PRESIDENT'S defense, the U.N. job seemed perfect for Bolton. Essentially a ceremonial position, it comes with only two responsibilities: to say whatever the president tells you to say and, when an official dinner is scheduled, to look good in a tuxedo. To be sure, the last task could prove difficult for the man, a thickish sort who wears his hair in the seductive style of a 1970s engineering student (with matching go-hither mustache). But this was not seen as insurmountable.

Nor did the exhaustive vetting process raise any concerns. FBI agents, assigned the routine task of conducting background checks on the nominee, found nothing unexpected, although neighbors did report seeing him foam at the mouth with some frequency. But agents explained this as simply an allergic reaction to Kofi Annan.

Even Bolton's colleagues at the State Department eagerly supported his promotion to New York City—"the sooner the better"—and many even offered to use personal leave to help him pack.

For her part, Rice hoped the nomination would proceed without delay, and had begun to wistfully imagine her new life without John Bolton: no more secret meetings in bathrooms to avoid his forceful counsel; no more awkward requests for subordinates to "take John to the zoo or something" during substantive conference calls; no more fashioning elaborate excuses to keep him out of sight from foreign dignitaries ("Sorry, John, but I really need the three-hole binders, not the two-hole type. Do you mind going back to Staples and exchanging them?").

THE SENATE VOTE on the Bolton nomination was delayed because senators were embroiled in a filibuster crisis over judicial nominations. Some feared that the Republican majority—in an effort to permanently suspend this traditional minority tactic of continuing debate despite majority wishes to the contrary—would deploy what has been called the "nuclear" option. This puzzled House Majority Leader Tom DeLay, who feels that conventional weapons (such as bribing legislators with trips abroad) usually produce better results. ∎

I'm Okay, You're Not

The staff at my office recently took the Myers-Briggs personality profile test and discovered that, surprisingly, many of us have actual personalities. The test is designed to help people understand that disagreements often occur because different personalities see things in different ways, and not because some people are wrong. In my case, however, it's because other people are wrong. Nonetheless, I cooperated fully with the test and was hopeful that the rest of the staff could finally learn how to improve themselves. I've been very patient.

The tests were useful in many ways, and not just because we got to sit at the big conference table and eat donuts while we filled them out. The exercise reminded us that there are indeed two sides to every issue (or, as I helpfully pointed out, "my way or the highway"), and that if we understand this simple principle most disagreements don't have to deteriorate into emotional battles. Of course, what's the fun of working in an office if you can't have emotional battles? ("I was NOT chewing bubble gum during my annual review! By the way, do you think an ice cube would help get that stuff out of my mustache?")

The test asks a series of carefully worded questions designed to determine the unique personality traits that make us who we are, such as:

- Are you comfortable in groups?
- At a party, would you describe yourself as funny and interesting?
- Those people who don't find you funny and interesting... is there, like, something wrong with them, or what?

The professional who interpreted the results of our tests was very helpful as she explained our different personality types. (I'm an Extroverted Intuitive Feeling Perceiving person, or ENFP, which is a really good personality type. So I think I won.) Then she said it's not about winning or losing, but about understanding yourself. (But, when pressed, she admitted she wasn't an ENFP herself, so I'm sensing a little envy here. We ENFPs get that a lot.)

Actually, knowing how personality affects relationships is helpful on more than just an interpersonal level. Take China and the United States, for example. Their "personalities" could not be more different: In China, the government is run by a president who is not chosen by a process of fair and honest elections. Whereas, in the United States our president almost always is. Sort of.

In China, the real power resides in the hands of a bloated and self-serving military. In our country, power resides with the people (which are defined by the Constitution as "bloated and self-serving wealthy donors"). In China, the government has very strict birth control laws to control the population. By contrast, the U.S. government decided years ago to stay out of our bedrooms (ever since it got caught hiding under the beds and giggling inappropriately).

ANYWAY, YOU GET THE IDEA. But if you don't, I'll try to talk slower since you're probably one of those "other" personality types. Let me put it this way: If China and the United States were symbolized by two people, then the U.S. would be the husband sitting in a comfy chair holding the remote control. China would be the wife wearing a cone-shaped straw hat and working very hard around the house. Plus, she rides a bicycle most of the time and talks real fast in a language he doesn't understand.

Clearly, they don't see "eye-to-eye." But it's simply because their personality types make them see things differently. The husband sees the glass as half empty (when he looks up during commercials). The wife sees the glass as an entry point to the World Trade Organization. She also sees the glass as an unacceptable justification for the United States' free-trade agreement with Taiwan.

Obviously, she's a very complicated person that her husband doesn't understand. But then he probably shouldn't have dated exchange students in the first place (it's not like the guys in his dorm didn't warn him about it).

Actually, differences of perspective can often be a "win-win" situation for those involved. For example, environmentalists were outraged when President Bush insisted we put the arsenic back in our drinking water. On the other hand, 7-Eleven applauded the decision and promptly announced its new line of delicious Zesty Arsenic Slurpees.

You see? Win-win. ∎

Turning 50: Surely, There Must Be Some Mistake...

The breakfast table was covered with birthday cards decoratively labeled "50," which meant somebody in our home had crossed the half-century mark. But who, I asked myself, gingerly rubbing ointment into muscles still inflamed from strenuous physical effort of getting out of bed.

Who is this aging person, I asked again, as I absent-mindedly hummed the theme song from "The Donna Reed Show."

Attempting to solve the mystery, I finally narrowed it down to either our 16-year-old daughter or myself. And since most 50-year-olds don't badger their parents to let them practice driving (at a place that used to have bushes growing alongside the road), I deduced that it must be...me.

(Actually, I think my Dad was 50 when he taught me how to drive. He was in his 40s when I got behind the wheel and two hours later he looked 50. But maybe it was because I always kept my hands at the 9 and 11 o'clock positions on the steering wheel, a technique I invented myself, which makes it easier to jump out of the car if the driver feels he can no longer take responsibility for the vehicle.)

Being 50 means I was born in the '40s, for gosh sakes! World War II was just over, and we had yet to get the bill for the Marshall Plan. (Congress: "This seems a little high. Couldn't they have used cheaper drywall or something?") I was born before rock 'n' roll, before StoveTop Stuffing. Ward and June Cleaver weren't even dating yet.

Why, if I really am 50, don't I look graying and distinguished, like Marlin Perkins of TV's "Wild Kingdom"? I use him as an example only because I actually met him when I was 9 years old. It was in the bathroom at the St. Louis Zoo, where he was curator, and he just walked in, like a regular person. I remember that as we stood together two things came to my mind: He was very tall, and, sometime earlier in the day, he must have been very thirsty.

It's bad enough knowing that at 50, almost a third of my life has passed. But what is more demoralizing is that I may never reach the primary goal of my youth. I have not been— and may never be—a guest on "The Johnny Carson Show."

I was recently reminded of my new status when, while being chased down an alley by a speeding UPS truck, I tripped and fell, disgorging the contents of my shirt pocket which, 30 years ago, would have consisted of an old movie ticket stub, a two-year-old unused condom (Boy Scout motto: Be prepared... like YOU got a chance, Four-Eyes!), and a fake ID with several miss-spellings. But being a 50-year-old, I'm required by law to carry reading glasses, a variety of pens, a newspaper clipping about calcium replacement, and a Things I Have To Do Today notebook. (I double-checked later and nowhere did it say, "Get hit by a UPS truck.") When I was young we never carried a notebook to keep track of our plans since, if I remember correctly, we didn't have any. We weren't like the kids today, who have a world of opportunity available in return for just the slightest effort, but which they never do on account of they have to check their e-mail.

IF I'D BEEN HIT BY that UPS truck before my latest birthday, my friends would have lamented my pitifully premature death, and spoken solemnly about how much more I could have given to the world. But now that I'm 50, they won't do that anymore. They'd just say how very sad it is, but point out that "well, after all, he was 50."

Physically, things start to change when you reach this milestone. For one thing, you have to start using the phrase "back in my day." For another, the statute of limitations for self-confidence has lapsed and it's time to start feeling bad about your body. So you join a gym.

Ironically, considering I'm paying to be there to feel better about myself, a gym does horrible things for my self-esteem. It takes about six months of hard work to get anywhere, and in the meantime, I feel like Calista Flockhart at a sumo wrestlers' convention. I'm surrounded by guys who only use the word "50" when referring to push-ups. They're so big that if Jane Goodall stopped by she would try to communicate with them. These guys are so huge that on the weekend they work for the U.S. Forest Service. As trees. (Editor's Note: ENOUGH already!)

I briefly had a personal trainer, but that didn't work out since the only phrases he knew in English were "give me five more!" or "who said you can stop now, miss?"

But that's okay. After a few minutes I get into my "zone" lifting heavy iron and doing half-squats. (Half squats is where you go down, but have to have help getting back up.) To pass the time I plu into my portable eight-track—that sits on its own easy-to-move gurney—and listen to the latest hit from Gary Lewis and the Playboys. Only to be interrupted by a trainer who comes over and tells me that I had, rather loudly, just asked the whole room if they wanted to "buy-uy-uy, this diamond ring-ing-ing-ing?" Answer: "Please don't sing, sir."

And speaking of embarrassment, I hate that turning 50 means you have to start getting complicated-sounding medical tests that end with the word "probe." Fortunately, knowing this could unnerve some patients, my shealth provider has designed a simple screening questionnaire for us older men:

1. Do you feel better than Boris Yeltzin (who is currently dead)?

2. If you answered "yes," please leave.

Don't get me wrong. I'm not implying that HMOs don't want you to live a long, healthy life. But if you can't, then please die quickly, and don't bother them. It's none of their business.

Actually, my last visit to the HMO went pretty smoothly until a nurse insisted—rather rudely, I felt—that I put my clothes back on. "Please, sir. You're still in the waiting room." ▪

Thar They Blow...

December, 2005

I s there anyone in this country who doesn't believe the recent hurricanes were caused by the oil companies? I didn't think so. They probably used a standard off-the-shelf Hurricane Death Ray invented by a mad scientist. You know the guy: brilliant, eccentric, still angry about having to go to the prom with his mother. He tested out of most classes in college then got hired by Texaco to develop a secret drug that gives auto executives a rash when they hear the words "better gas mileage."

To be fair, it's possible the scientist isn't really mad. Maybe he's just a decent man who does evil things because oil executives tied his daughter to a railroad track.

Of course, none of this is mentioned in the recent full-page newspaper ad—"Progress Report from ExxonMobil"—which stated that the company is "working hard" to get their refineries back on line after the hurricanes. Oil executives even gave a news conference and promised to "get right on it." But when they left the podium I noticed they were taking baby steps— you know, heel-toe, heel-toe—and smiling. Definitely smiling.

For its part, petroleum giant BP (an acronym for "Better PR") promised to boldly continue using the color green in its ads.

In the meantime, gas is hovering around $3 a gallon, a far

cry from the days when my dad, before he mowed the yard, would send me to the corner service station with a gallon gas can and a quarter. "And bring back the change," he would add, only too aware of the mischief an 11-year-old could get into with an extra 7 cents in his pocket.

THE HURRICANES MAY have subsided, but the winds of blame still blow in the nation's capital. And the only thing the federal government can point to with pride is FEMA's new Third Responders program: "We don't get there first. We don't get there second. But right after that we get there. Usually."

Fortunately, congressional Republicans have moved quickly and are holding hearings to determine exactly who wasn't to blame, and to identify by name who will not be held responsible. "If this leads to a public vindication, so be it," said one Republican lawmaker, off the record, for fear of being accused of clearing his name prematurely.

Congress was following the strong example set by President Bush who, immediately after the first hurricane, set his jaw and declared a global war on hurricanism. No stranger to courageous resolve, he then promised a rapid federal response in rebuilding the storm-ravaged areas, starting with Trent Lott's porch and Mississippi's casinos. Asked by reporters about the displacement of New Orleans' poor people, Bush replied, simply, "Mission accomplished," though panicked White House aids later explained that the president was reading from the wrong briefing book. (It was then that pundits wondered if the crisis was testing Bush's mettle, but few could explain what a mettle actually is and, if tested, whether it would get you into a good college.)

To reassure the public, the president named Karl Rove to be White House point man for the recovery, knowing that his political adviser would aggressively tackle a tragedy that had displaced thousands of swing voters. Rove pledged to "spare no effort to clear my name.... Oops...I mean to help those who find themselves investigated by independent counsels... oops, sorry again. (This is going to take some practice.)"

Elsewhere in Washington, D.C.:

- House Minority Leader Nancy Pelosi, in a welcome display of nonpartisanship, insisted that hurricane victims should receive immediate financial assistance, as soon as they filled out voter registration forms.

- Senate Majority Leader Bill Frist, after viewing a video of the disaster, said he definitely thinks New Orleans is alive and well, but couldn't be sure until he had time to get his feet on the ground and see which way the wind is blowing. A spokesperson said this is to determine whether conservative Christians are for or against hurricanes, and whether any stem cells were injured in the floods.

- The State Department announced that other nations have offered aid but that hey, we don't need anybody's help because, in case you forgot, we're the Number One superpower in the world! Well, except in education, health care, infant mortality, and pretty much any other social indicator of quality of life for the non-rich. (I meant that we're Number One in military sales. My bad.)

- The Department of Homeland Security recommended that a czar be appointed to oversee the recovery, and President Bush said he would find the best person for the job, "someone close to me, someone I can trust." So far, he has settled on either his longtime driver or a guy he just met in the lobby. (But this time I hope we get a real czar, you know, a guy that sits on a golden throne with a falcon on his shoulder. Now THAT'S a czar.) ∎

To Grandmother's House We Go

Our yearly trips to see Great Grandma have always been bittersweet. From the time the children were very young, we have told them to savor each visit, since the frail and feeble relative would probably be going to meet Jesus very soon.

That was four presidents ago.

Today, at age 95, Grandma has outlived two husbands, numerous suitors, and every major appliance in her house. And the only way she'll meet Jesus is if he shows up at her nursing home with a deck of cards and some pocket change he doesn't mind losing.

This year she greeted us with two questions: "Who are you?" and "Did you bring any beer?" After patiently explaining our identities (her reply: "Suit yourself"), we began the most important task at hand: cleaning out her purse. Aside from card-playing, Grandma's other pastime is sneaking food from the dining room, which she apparently does just for sport, since she never actually eats the donuts and creamers that we find mingled with the rosaries, rubber bands, and old get-well cards from people concerned about her health. (Grandma always gets better and later attends most of their funerals.)

Grandma has lived in three nursing homes in the last 10 years, each change prompted by management that felt she'd "be much happier elsewhere." The real reason, of course, is that other residents don't appreciate the little "whoop whoop" sound she makes every time she lays down her cards and reminds them that they probably shouldn't have skipped their nap that day.

HALF THE FUN of visiting Grandma is staying with the cousins in the rural outskirts of this little town, where people say strange, rural-oriented things like "Can I borrow your bulldozer?" This year their teen-age son alerted his friends that two city girls were coming, and soon after we arrived we could see the dust rising from fast-moving vehicles in the distance. In a few minutes three pick-up trucks stopped in front and disgorged five teen-age boys with John Deere caps on their heads and big grins on their faces. Obviously, from a parent's point of view, they could not be trusted.

They came to see my daughters, but you wouldn't know it from their behavior, which consisted mainly of hitting each other repeatedly on the upper arms and arguing about which was better: Ford or Chevy. The discussion was a spirited one, with the Ford owners aggressively pointing out the superior qualities of their vehicle, and concluding with a short list of waste products that Chevy owners are full of. Chevy owners then substantiated their own claims, and pointed out that Ford owners, coincidentally, were also full of the same substances.

This went on for, oh, about three hours, the truck comparisons taking on a degree of specificity not generally appreciated by the lay person. Or teen-age girls, for that matter, who remained with the boys not out of interest in the topic—they had none—but because of some unspoken species loyalty. It was either that or go inside with the parents, one of whom was conspicuously peering out of the garage window.

Eventually the daughters came in the house (giving me barely enough time to run from the window and leap onto the couch, lest they think I was doing anything other than reading a magazine...upside-down). The girls eagerly informed me they'd been invited to "go muddin.'" They explained that this meant squeezing as many young people as possible into the cab of a pick-up that then follows other trucks at high speeds down dark country roads until they find a muddy field, where they then drive around in circles in a display of rural-oriented fun. When they tire of this, the young people pass around a celebratory 12-pack of beer, which they consume before driving home.

I quickly gave my permission—why shouldn't kids be allowed to have their fun, for gosh sakes?—the only stipulation being that a woolly mammoth must first come charging across a nearby field. My daughters immediately accused me of sarcasm (moi?), but in my defense I pointed out that the giant mammal was, in fact, indigenous to this area a few short millennia ago. A sighting was unlikely, but I felt there was at least a remote statistical possibility.

Of course, if a woolly mammoth did appear on the horizon, the girls would probably rush into the house for a camera to record the event for an award-winning science project. The boys, with similar fast-thinking, would quickly begin debating which vehicle could best out-run a woolly mammoth: Ford or Chevy. ∎

Flu Season's Greetings

January, 2006

The Christmas season is a time of hope and expectation, a time of waiting: for the Christ child, for prophecy to be fulfilled, for severe muscle aches and a temperature of 104. This year, depending on your religious beliefs, Santa Claus may or may not be coming to town, but the bird flu definitely is, and it won't matter if you've been bad or good. It will be bad.

Every major international health organization, including our own Centers for Disease Control and Prevention (motto: THE SKY IS FALLING!), say that it is not a matter of if a pandemic will sweep the globe, but when. And those of you with the annoying habit of saying "bless you" at every sneeze will be of little help.

The virus started in Asia, where it can be produced more cheaply, and is slowly spreading west, following the ancient trade route established by a dispirited Marco Polo returning from the east with the bad news that his countrymen didn't, in fact, invent spaghetti. By April the virus could be in Paris, where fashion experts are predicting surgical masks will be all the rage.

Originating as a bird-borne disease, the virus spread first among the chicken farms of Vietnam, where poor farmers lived and even slept in close proximity to their flocks. (Don't laugh. You sleep with your dog, right? Which, in some Asian cultures, would be like taking a pot roast to bed.) Scientists don't know exactly how the avian flu virus mutates into a strain that can infect humans (personally, I blame teenagers), but members of the Kansas Board of Education were more confident, proclaiming that its mysterious complexity can mean only one thing: It was created by intelligent design. Turns out, if something's too complicated to easily understand, it must have come from the hand of God. (I'd like to take this moment to thank God for my Mr. Coffee. I don't know exactly how it works, but it's a real blessing in the morning.)

Fortunately, the Bush administration has been swift in its response to the viral threat, because—let's face it—the prospect of millions dying from the flu makes a great distraction from a really bad news month at the White House. Administration officials wisely decided the federal response should not repeat the mistakes made after Hurricane Katrina, a natural disaster that, because of a history of misplaced fiscal priorities and market-driven decisions, did far more damage than it should have. So the president has been brutally honest with the country regarding the coming pandemic, and told us that, because of a history of misplaced fiscal priorities and market-driven decisions, vaccines are no longer produced in sufficient quantity.

Thus, medicine will be rationed first to the elderly, then to the sick and infirm, which prompted former vice presidential chief of staff Lewis "Scooter" Libby to ask, "If you're in jail, can you qualify for a flu shot as, like, a shut-in?"

Actually, I'm not so sure I want a flu shot, since the last time I got one I immediately came down with flu. On the other hand, I got it over with right away. (Applying that same logic, to guarantee that your next family car trip is accident-free, make sure you back over the mailbox on the way out.) Apparently, I now qualify as elderly, since last week a waitress handed me the menu with the "Seniors Specials." But I sent her away with a youthful wave of my hand, telling her to mind her own business and bring me the chipped beef. (It's easier to chew.)

THE ECONOMIC IMPACT of the flu pandemic is not yet clear, although county fairs across the country have reportedly shut down their kissing booths, and candy manufacturers have postponed introduction of the new "Share-A-Lick" all-day sucker. Additionally, avian petting zoos across the nation are expected to close up shop. (Parent: "It's okay, honey, the bird's just sleeping." Kid, poking it with a stick, scientifically: "I don't think so, Mom. By the way, can I bring it home?")

For most of us, the best defense against the coming pandemic is to stay inside our homes for the duration of winter, where we'll be insulated by layers of unconscionably high heating bills stuffed into our mailbox. Because the oil industry is still working on its first $1 trillion profit, I'm using alternative means to heat my house. For example, I plan to put a toaster in the middle of my living room, and to always carry one of our cats when I get up to move around or to put another log in to toast. The cats are warm, soft, and, in one case, as big as a beanbag chair. (It's nice to know that finally there is another use for these pets besides just companionship. And meat.)

In the meantime, drink lots of fluids, exercise, and eat wisely. And this Christmas, keep your distance from the partridge in the pear tree. Especially if it sneezes. ∎

One Down...

This has been a year of major milestones for our family, not the least of which was the realization that I might finally be allowed to use our bathroom. After 17 years of mentoring and molding, we finally dropped off a child at college. Unfortunately, it was the wrong child, so we had to go back and drag our 15-year-old out of the dorm, scold her for impersonating her older sister, and demand to know what she had done with her.

But we got that straightened out, freed our eldest from her sister's closet where she had been left with food, water, and four Harry Potter books (which, our youngest reasoned, is all anyone really needs for survival), and shipped off the correct daughter to a small college in upstate New York. We chose this school for its rigorous academic tradition, its generous en-dowment, and for its long and harsh winters. The latter was important, we felt, since it would shorten the time our child walked around in her typical teen-ager attire which, in Greek mythology, would cause distraught sailors to plunge to their deaths in an effort to reach shore. We figured a couple winters in New York would turn her into a more sensible dresser, one who would not be mistaken for a pop star or a prostitute. (It's so hard to tell the difference these days. In my youth, you could always identify the former by their heavy make-up, flashy clothes, and garish wigs. Or am I thinking of Boy George?)

It seems like only yesterday that my spouse and I were saying to each other "We really should start saving for college." Unfortunately, it *was* only yesterday, which—and I say this with the conviction that only comes from meticulous and thoughtful planning—was WAY too late. Fortunately, our daughter worked very hard in high school and earned a nice financial aid "package." Not to mention President Bush's tax rebate, which will help a lot, as soon as we decide which book it will pay for.

Fortunately, our other child is already working hard to be eligible for a full college scholarship. For example, she's planning on doing very well on the Harry Potter portion of the SAT.

WITH OUR ELDEST OUT of the house, we can now focus all our time on our youngest daughter, even though she does not seem particularly grateful for this new development. She just doesn't appreciate how much easier it makes parenting when there's only one child in the house. Now we just have one person to frisk for drugs and firearms when she returns home, just one bed to look under for cigarettes, just one set of calls from boys to monitor from the upstairs extension (at least, until my daughter catches me with the phone in my hand. But I can tell her I was "just dusting").

And speaking of bathrooms, I had assumed that a one-third reduction in the female population would measurably limit the amount of pastel-colored debris that I had to walk around during my weekly shower. (I joined a gym years ago just to have a place to shave in the morning and only ONCE did I ever see anything pastel-colored on that floor. Okay, it was my Big Bird towel, but I stopped using it right after some big guys laughed at me after they snapped me with it accidentally.)

Unfortunately, the various gender-specific doohickies and

somethings-on-a-rope are going to remain in the tub since there is still no place to put them on the shelves above. These shelves are crowded with ointments, creams, and other liquids about which I know nothing, except that under no circumstances am I permitted to touch them. Not that I would want to bathe with anything containing actual chunks of apricots and asparagus (what, no balsamic vinegar?). No, I'm only allowed to use the leftover motel soaps my parents bring when they visit. They get them for free on their trips. (They've also offered us bedspreads and side tables, but the Best Western motif clashes with my decor. Plus, that would be WRONG, MOM AND DAD!)

Ironically, even after losing half the children, we still have ALL their pets. Colleges don't allow students to bring animals, since the football players are hard enough to clean up after. Fortunately, we only have two more years until our other daughter goes off to school, at which point we'll immediately send the pets back to wherever they came from. Presumably a destination arrived at via flushing.

(Okay, okay! I was just kidding about flushing. Anyhow, cats have a homing instinct and would eventually find their way back from the municipal water treatment plant.) ∎

Finally, an Immigration Solution

July, 2006

(Editor's note: Some of the following observations may be inappropriate by now, such as the sarcastic tone in which our nation's concern for immigrants was mocked. On the contrary, our nation welcomes all strangers, because, like it says on the Statue of Liberty, simply, "Bring me your cutest."
(Hey! Who painted that over?!)

Congress and the White House have yet to settle the contentious immigration debate that has consumed our nation in the fires of divisiveness, threatened the bulwark of our democracy, and turned brother against brother and father against sons.

Or maybe I'm thinking of the Civil War. Whatever.

Be that as it may, there's a clear reason it has taken so long for our political leaders to find a solution to this vexing issue: They didn't ask me.

I've had the answer for months now, and were it not for the distraction of the woefully unfair voting on American Idol—can you believe Katharine McPhee didn't win?! It's an OUTRAGE!—I could have stepped in and settled this once and for all.

Actually, it's quite simple: I believe that all immigrants

who have entered this country illegally should be sent home. No exceptions.

Just as soon as they finish all the projects we have for them.

This means, simply, that at the precise moment that our office buildings, hotels, and motels are cleaned for the final time, the immigrants who push those funny-looking carts around should immediately return to their home countries. Hasta la vista. (You just know they were taking toilet paper rolls that didn't belong to them.)

Just as soon as all our potholes are finally fixed and won't appear again (I can't WAIT!), the illegals that work on our streets in the boiling heat of summer and in the harsh winds of winter—I know they do this because I've often watched from my office window—they should just up and leave. Sayonara.

And just as soon as our bridges, schools, and the rest of our infrastructure are built and repaired, and this nation is finally bright and shiny and new, then we don't need those workers any more. At that moment, they will have officially overstayed their welcome. ("Welcome" being loosely translated as "stalked, threatened, hunted down, and generally treated as sub-human." That kind of welcome.)

In the meantime, we'll just have to put up with all of the problems associated with illegal immigrants, such as inexpensive labor, an uncompromising work ethic, and the billions of dollars* in productivity they contribute annually.

We'll have to put up with the fact that they are keeping our food prices low, our lawns cared for, and our homes painted and repaired for a reasonable price. Not to mention that most of them are doing a heckuva job which, in the nation's capital, can get you, like, the Medal of Freedom.

And it won't be easy for our society to cope with the children of immigrants, as they grow up in households where hard work and sacrifice are the norm and paychecks are often sent to needy relatives. That kind of role model could cause an unexpected cultural shift that would undermine traditional American values, which guide our children through their formative years of text-messaging, shopping, and developing critical brand loyalties. After all, our kids know where their self-worth comes from, and it's not from some cheap iPod. Nope. It's from the more expensive iPod, the one that holds up to 5,000 songs!

In raising my own children—mainly during commercials— I would try to instill the important values that form the backbone of a productive society. But then the show would come back on and I'd have to stop. So I guess they picked up that values stuff somewhere else. Maybe at the mall.

I'M WELL AWARE that my solution to the immigration crisis is a controversial one, and it has not come without risk to my personal reputation. Recently, in fact, a group of retired generals has publicly called for my resignation. (Or am I thinking of somebody else?) But I am undeterred. In fact, in an effort to draw the attention of government authorities to my innovative ideas, I recently enriched uranium in my office.

Admittedly, it's a small amount, nothing like what's giving Iran the kind of bragging rights that any high school chemistry major would envy. But it's enough to be taken seriously by international monitoring groups and ... excuse me ... "CARE-FULWITHTHAT! Easy. Easy. Now put it back in the mini-fridge where you found it." (Nosey colleagues.)

Actually, it's been hard to keep track of the stuff, because somebody comes in my office every night and cleans up the place. I wonder who does that? Elves, maybe. ∎

Arresting Development

(Editor's note: By now, the convicted criminals discussed below have probably been rehabilitated, released from prison, and launched promising careers in the Christian ministry or on Dancing with the Stars.)

Setting a high moral tone for the coming year, elected officials have extended the traditional Christmas spirit by spontaneously contributing thousands of dollars to charity. Admittedly, most of the money was from confessed criminal lobbyist Jack Abramoff, but this should not detract from the fact that members of Congress wanted to send a powerful message of charity to the American people, many of whom might one day serve on their juries.

Abramoff was first to get things started when he returned from a Christmas season spent a-wassailing (an Old English phrase that means "meeting with my lawyers") and announced that his New Year's resolution is to fully cooperate with federal prosecutors in their probe of bribery and influence peddling on Capitol Hill. In pleading guilty to numerous felony counts, he left many members of Congress trembling with, I'm guessing, admiration. Anyway, they were trembling.

Abramoff voluntarily appeared in court after his lawyers patiently explained that his career was similar to—but not nearly as pleasant as—toast.

Thus, Abramoff stood before a judge, wearing the best suit Native American casino money can buy, and pleaded for leniency. (Note: Since one of the charges against him is under-reporting income on his tax forms, he will no doubt be declaring the cost of that suit at, say, $6 million or so, if he can just find the receipt. Unfortunately, Abramoff also forgot to write off some of his other legitimate purchases, such as the House of Representatives.)

Among the charges to which Abramoff admitted guilt are tax evasion, corruption, bribery, and, most seriously, giving the word "scoundrel" a bad name.

A chastened Abramoff told the judge the following: "I just want to say that words will not ever be able to express my sorrow and my profound regret for all my actions and mistakes." (Translation: "Since words can't express my sorrow to you, your honor, how about a new car?") He went on to add, "For all my remaining days, I will feel tremendous sadness and regret for what I have done. I only hope that I can merit forgiveness from the Almighty and from those I have wronged or caused to suffer." (Translation: "This is gonna hurt, isn't it?")

Attempts at contacting the Almighty were not successful, but a spokesperson from the other side of the aisle—Satan—admitted that he was unprepared for the severity of Abramoff's crimes. "Somehow this guy was completely off our radar screen, and we're having to seriously rethink what to do with him. I mean, he's really lowered the bar, and frankly I'm starting to worry about my job. He's just too good. I mean... bad."

After his multiple guilty pleas in Washington, D.C., Abramoff then flew to Miami to plead guilty to defrauding lenders during the purchase of 20 casino boats. For the sake of fairness, it's still not clear whether Abramoff wanted the boats to help victims of Hurricane Katrina or—more likely—he planned to board each boat with a Bible in one hand and a whip in the other and personally drive out the gamblers and charlatans that had turned these humble crafts into floating pleasure palaces of sin. HALLELUJAH!

Despite his many legal troubles, there was a bright spot. A judge recently cleared Abramoff of suspicion in the gangland-style murder of his Florida business partner, a move that should help establish the strength of his moral character when it comes time for sentencing. Legal experts confirmed that judges usually go a little easier on defendants who don't kill people gangland-style.

REPORTEDLY, ABRAMOFF'S greatest crime was bribing members of Congress. But before we get down on congressman let's be honest: who among us could turn down one of his all-expenses-paid golfing trips to Scotland where, against the backdrop of the beautiful mist-shrouded coasts, one pictures Tom DeLay complaining loudly that his slice is still just as bad as it was on that crummy public course next to the landfill in East Texas. (DeLay: "How can I concentrate on my drive with ALL THIS MIST!?")

Washington pundits are now saying that, because of his involvement in the scandals, DeLay's political career is DeFunct, and he may even have trouble resuming his old job as exterminator back home in Texas. Others disagree, saying that DeLay is now even more qualified to clear out a house full of vermin. "What self-respecting pest would want to be in the same room as this guy?"

Meanwhile, in an effort to reform themselves and regain the public trust, elected officials from both parties have enrolled in ethics classes which, among other things, teach the difference between a gift and a bribe. (Answer: It depends on how gullible the judge is.) The class also employs the use of flash cards printed with new words like "integrity," "honesty," and "minimizing prison time." ∎

To Your Health

My office recently changed over to a different health insurance company. The new company is less expensive than our previous insurer, and it covers virtually every pre-existing medical condition except stuttering. ("No, I swear I never stuttered before I signed up. I just walked in here, and, well, it s-s-s-s-ort of came over me all at once.")

Our new insurance company seems pretty good. At least the application (below) was only one page long. The only thing I wondered about is a new procedure—called a "group x-ray"—that the staff has to get once a year. Apparently it saves the insurance company a lot of money, but I don't see how we're all going to fit on that table at one time.

But seriously, health care is an important concern of all Americans, particularly sick people who wish they lived in virtually any other industrialized nation except ours. Here in the United States, if you go to a hospital you pray that your insurance is accepted—otherwise you're put on the "standby stretcher" (the one with rust on the wheels), and you have to share a bed pan with somebody you don't know.

With all the conflicting opinions about our nation's health crisis, it's nice to hear at least one clear voice of integrity. Not surprisingly, it's from cigarette executives, the people who have the courage to state that their products have absolutely nothing to do with health. In fact, there is very little evidence linking cigarettes to lung cancer, and as soon as that's shredded and burned there won't be any at all.

But seriously, you have to feel sorry for cigarette executives, after U.S. senators mercilessly accused them of targeting young people with new tobacco products. Indignant company spokespersons denied the charges, claiming that no one could prove the new Barney's Playtime Menthol 100s were aimed at children. Nor, they insist, is there anything wrong with the new advertising jingle: "I love you, you love me, so let's go smoke a cigarette."

Well-Co Insurance, Inc.
The company that says: Don't get sick. No, really, don't get sick.
— SERVING HEALTHY PEOPLE SINCE 1988 —

APPLICATION FOR INSURANCE
The following E-Z questionnaire is designed to give us a general idea of your medical history. Our policy is to insure absolutely everyone who applies, regardless of any pre-existing conditions. Unless they're sick.

1. Do you have any germs? _Yes _ No
If Yes, please list them:

2. Give a brief description of every time you have ever been sick in your entire life. (Use additional sheets of paper, if necessary).

3. Do you smoke cigarettes? _ Yes _ No
If "yes," are you, like, a moron or something? Please list any other suicidal tendencies you may have:

4. Which of the following foods have you eaten in the last 24 hours?

a. Raw vegetables

b. Oat bran

c. A large bag of Frito-Lard's Deep-Fried Pork Parts (If you circled "c", please discontinue filling out this form and immediately contact the nearest medical school who will be happy to accept your body for scientific research, in the very near future.)

5. Which of the following best describes your exercise regimen?

a. I walk at least five miles a week.

b. I ride a stationary bicycle for 30 minutes a day.

c. I keep my ice cream at a neighbor's house, so I have to walk a lot during commercials.

d. Could you repeat the question? You see, I get these dizzy spells...

6. How many fingers am I holding up? _Two _Three _Yes

And finally:

7. Do you expect any payments from this insurance company?

_ No

_ *Heavens* no! If I get sick or injured it's probably my fault and I shouldn't expect anybody else to be responsible. This is America, and that just wouldn't be right. ∎

English, the One and Only

August, 2006

I n accordance with the recent Senate action that would make English our national language, I have decided not to write this piece in classical Greek, a linguistic expression with which I'm more comfortable. (I just love those Greek letters on fraternity houses, although it turns out they all mean the same thing: "Beer inside.") Despite this inconvenience, however, I am convinced that the Senate—our most deliberative body—knew what it was doing when it courageously recognized the obvious, and then acted forcefully to show it was paying attention.

In other prescient measures, the Senate also ruled that water is wet and that broccoli sometimes gets stuck in your teeth and looks unsightly.

All that remains for English to become the requisite language of the land is for the House of Representatives—our least deliberative body—to approve the measure without requiring non-English speakers to be dragged from their homes and taken some place unpleasant. I'm not saying this would happen, but there's something about the House that makes its members act a little wacky. (Which explains why the Founding Fathers originally called it the House of Doofuses, a little known fact.)

Tom DeLay, for example, was just a simple Texas extermi-nator when he came to the House of Representatives, and now look at him. He's discredited, under indictment, and taking the last refuge of scoundrels: Jesus, whom he plans to represent in his new job as Christian lobbyist. In that role DeLay will be pushing a more biblical agenda on Capitol Hill, starting with more tax cuts for the rich, because that's just what Jesus would do. (We know this because it's right there in the Bible, some-place. Maybe in the back.)

ALREADY THE SENATE'S action is having a broad impact. As you know, Iran is developing weapons of mass destruction (we know this because the CIA says so, and they're never wrong about such things). To distract attention from the nuclear build-up, Iran's president wrote a long personal letter to our Reader-In-Chief, President Bush. And it was in English.

Mahmoud Ahmadinejad did not send the letter in his na-tive language because he knew that American translators wouldn't get past his letterhead, much less the rest of his mis-sive. (By my count, the Iranian president's name contains no fewer than 16 consonants—all of which are silent, for fear of reprisals—and another dozen vowels. Plus, if you write it backwards it spells "Constantinople." Twice.)

While his 20-page polemic compared our great nation to Satan—which would have been laughable had he not used some pretty persuasive footnotes—it failed to address an issue much more important to Americans: namely, that Ah-madinejad looks exactly like a young Bob Denver. (Skipper, after stepping on a rake carelessly left in front of his tent: "AH-MADINEGILLIGAN!!")

The Iranian president isn't the only one to recognize the su-periority of our native tongue. Attorney General Alberto Gon-zales, the son of Mexican immigrants, has found his adopted language particularly invaluable when giving vague and circuitous answers at congressional hearings. English is perfect for this, since his native Spanish does not have a word for obfuscation. ("Obfuscanado" might work, but I think it's also the name of that funky 1960s car with the pick-up truck back-end.)

And only in English could White House officials glibly announce that "when adjusted for inflation, gas prices are still at historic lows." If you said that in any other language you'd hear the sharp barking laughter of non-English-speaking economists. But what do they know?

I WAS AT FIRST skeptical about being confined to a single language, since I frequently use the non-native ixnay when scolding wayward colleagues. But that was before I attended a high school opera recital, which for some reason they were singing in Italian. Or possibly German. Hopefully this new law will put a stop to this.

After all, opera is hard enough to follow (what with all the singing), and it took a kindly friend to explain that it usually consists of two major themes: spurned love—predominately by servant girls towards their employers—or abandonment by God. The latter was hard to believe in this case since the singers wore gowns and tuxedos. (If the guys had been singing in gowns, then I'd buy the bit about God abandoning them. And credit God for a great sense of humor.)

I have nothing against people singing their feelings in operas, or on high school dates for that matter, although I can tell you from personal experience that some people are less receptive to the latter. Elvis Presley—perhaps our greatest English speaker—pulled this off memorably when singing his love to Ann-Margret in *Viva, Las Vegas!*, a touching romantic film that showed the emotional bonds a man and a woman can achieve by singing at each other—at point-blank range—in English. But maybe that only happens in places outside the United States, like Nevada. ∎

First Day on the Job

September, 2006

Congratulations to Abu Hamza al-Muhajir, the new head of al Qaeda in Iraq. It's a challenging job, but he clearly has the right stuff to lead, such as knowing which end of the gun the bullets come out of. We mention this only because apparently this fact was not known to his predecessor, Abu Musab "Big Al" al-Zarqawi, who was shown in a video requiring assistance from henchpersons so that he wouldn't accidentally shoot off a toe. (It's hard to inspire allegiance from international jihadists when you shoot yourself in the foot. Somebody else's foot, maybe. But not your own.)

President George W. Bush immediately gave al-Muhajir the official United States seal of approval by publicly announcing he is "on our list to bring to justice." That pretty much makes al-Muhajir the poster boy for thousands of young men in the Islamist world, so heckofajob, Mr. President. (White House officials privately conceded their relief at having a new face of evil in Iraq. They hadn't had one since Dick Cheney left after his last visit.)

In case the world had any doubts about the virility and resolve of the new terrorist leader, a photo recently released by al-Jazeera ("All the news that really annoys Americans") shows al-Muhajir firing an AK-47 outfitted with an extra large ammunition magazine. He didn't come right out and say it, but his message was clear: "My ammo clip is bigger than your ammo clip." The photo also revealed that al-Muhajir is quite the man of fashion, cutting an impressive figure in his slate gray skullcap with matching boot-cut pants, accented by a dark beige bullet-proof vest. Terrorism is not pretty, but nobody said it has to be ugly.

Al-Muhajir's first day on the job was probably typical of what any new hire would experience at the office. First on the itinerary is finding out where the office supplies are kept; you know, copy paper, Post-it notes, rocket-propelled grenades. And then he met with his staff:

Intern: We who are about to die salute you.

Al-Muhajir: Well said, young man.

Intern: Actually, it's from *Gladiator*. Russell Crowe is, like, my favorite actor.

At my office we celebrate a new employee's first day by serving bagels and coffee in the lunchroom. Then we go outside and, in typical American non-profit fashion, we fire our Kalashnikov rifles into the air. Sometimes we get carried away and forget to hurry back inside, which means getting bonked on the head when the bullets fall back down. It's really funny when that happens.

No doubt al-Muhajir was similarly welcomed by his colleagues. Although we heard it got a little scary when an overly enthusiastic new recruit, not wanting to be left out of the celebration, tried to set off his own explosive vest. Fortunately, it was quickly pointed out to him that this might defeat the purpose of the event, which was definitely not to turn the new boss into little al Qaeda bits.

WE DON'T KNOW what qualifications al-Muhajir brings to his new job, or why he was chosen over other equally ambitious al-Wannabes. Maybe he caught the attention of al-Zarqawi by bringing him coffee and newspapers each morning. Or maybe he displayed initiative by painting a large bull's-eye on the roof of his boss's house. (It was just his way of reaching out to the new Iraqi government or, more specifically, the American fighter-bombers circling overhead.) Regardless, he got the job and he's ready to continue the work, even though the job description is pretty vague. After all, al-Muhajir has little precedent to follow since al Qaeda didn't arrive until AFTER the U.S. invasion, Mr. Vice President!

Sorry.

Al-Muhajir's first order of business, as he attempts to establish rapport with his colleagues and collaborators is that he is, under absolutely no circumstances, to be mistaken for a Sunni. Or, for that matter a Shia, depending on the neighborhood. Let's face it, it's not easy being a terrorist when you're constantly avoiding sectarian animosities. "The violence is just so random and purposeless," the new al Qaeda leader was overheard saying. "It's getting so I can't go anywhere for fear of being blown up because I'm in the wrong religion. What IS it with these nuts?!"

I can understand his frustration. Sectarian rivalry was rampant in my own life when I was a young Southern Baptist. I remember my Sunday school class used to go downtown and hurl sacramental grape juice at the Northern Baptists. We were incensed because they ... umm ... I forget what they did, but it was definitely a heretical abomination. Fortunately, I gave up such caustic prejudices when I became an adult and would never think of hurling grape juice at anybody, unless it would improve their general appearance. (Karl Rove comes to mind, for some reason.) ∎

Little-Known Fact:

There are Vampire Interns in Washington, D.C.

The battle was over almost before it began. The Armies of Darkness knew they had no chance against the legendary warrior as he stared down at them from his powerful horse, his hair blowing majestically in the wind (the warrior's hair, not the horse's). As he surveyed the vanquished field below, the great warrior sheathed his sword for the final time. "I will fight no more," he thought to himself as he took a moist towelette from his utility belt and wiped the dust of battle from his bifocals.

And then I woke up.

It must have been the voices murmuring from the other side of the room.

"Is he dead?"

"Nah. He's just sleeping."

"But it's the middle of the afternoon!"

"Yeah, well, he's kinda old."

They were office interns, interrupting my afternoon power nap, a nap I find increasingly necessary these days as my biological clock requires frequent rewinding. But what do interns know, these people of perpetual youth who leave after a year for some dark and secret place where their life forces are restored and their bodies given new forms for their return.

They are ageless and forever young. They are the undead. Vampires.

OKAY, SO MAYBE they're not vampires. It just seems that way because I think I'm the only one getting old around here. And having crossed the middle-age threshold, I'm not sure I'm quite ready to move on to the next exciting phase of life: Fearing Death.

Fortunately, death is not a new topic for me. Even as a young child I expressed an interest in the subject by frequently lying in front of a full-length mirror in the den and closing my eyes. Then I would open them ever so slightly to see what I would look like if I were dead. (I would lay there, eyes fluttering, until the dog came up and just sat there, drooling expectantly.) But I don't do that anymore, mainly because all our mirrors are up high, and my daughters don't like it when I lay across their dresser with my eyes partially closed. They think it's creepy.

It might be the funerals I've been attending lately that have created this new preoccupation. It hasn't helped that the deceased have been people not all that much older than myself. Fortunately, I'm there as the guitar player, so I can maintain a certain emotional detachment from the event. (Not that I mind being there, since I'm always looking for more venues to perform. Just not with so many flowers.)

Frankly, I'm over-qualified for funerals, and I seldom get to share the music that I am most prepared to play. For example, "Stairway to Heaven" is, in my opinion, the perfect send-off song for a funeral. But people just stare blankly at me when I suggest it, like it was a bad idea or something.

But it's more than the unfortunate song choices that bothers me about funerals. I've noticed that these events also suffer from a noticeable lack of perspective. I realize that it's a funeral, but the eulogies of a life well-lived seem to cry out for balance. I mean, would a brief time of rebuttal be that disrespectful? Wouldn't it be refreshing just once, in the middle of the appreciations, to hear someone stand up and say, "Well, yes, he had a great life, but I remember this one weekend when we were on a road trip and...."

I DO NOT FEAR death. I believe most of the things promised in the books of the New Testament, not including Revelation, which predicts unnecessarily large quantities of trumpets, a musical instrument that I personally feel should be used sparingly.

I believe in Heaven, and your assorted Mansions in the Sky. And I believe in the Chariots of Fire with their special tires that don't damage the Streets of Gold. It all sounds good, but I'm in no hurry. In fact, I've given specific instructions for my family to keep me around as long as possible. There'll be no pulling the plug on me, no sir. "Spare no expense" is my motto for hanging around, at least until a medical procedure can be developed that allows my family to donate their major organs in as painless a way as possible. After all, I'm concerned about them, too.

But when I do pass on, I ask only for the simplest of memorial services, to be preceded by a brief month of public mourning and no more than a week of me lying in state. And when the mourning has regrettably subsided, my ashes are to be sprinkled, with appropriate ceremony, over the breakfast cereal of former congressman Tom DeLay.

And don't tell him. I want it to be a surprise. ∎

Newt Gingrich: He's Back!

(Editor's Note: The following was written in March of 2007, well before the 2008 presidential campaign was in full swing and Newt Gingrich's was regularly denying he was running. In the coming months, however, he would continue to press his rehabilitation campaign as a commentator on various major news programs...I'm sorry, but I can't BELIEVE people are still listening to this guy!)

In the past year, while you were avoiding public service by selfishly living from paycheck to paycheck, former Speaker of the House Newt Gingrich has appeared on numerous news shows pledging to move our nation forward with brand new ideas, such as electing him president, though he strongly denies he's running. (Coincidentally, neither am I, since I'm spending my time living paycheck to paycheck.)

This is the same guy who, because of ethics violations while in office, used to be called the Disgraced Former Speaker. Apparently, he's been waiting for the right political moment, quietly biding his time, like one of those crocodiles whose alert eyes are visible above murky waters, while the rest of his large reptilian body lies just beneath the surface. I'm not saying he personally has a large reptilian body, at least not like, depending on your angle of view, Dennis Hastert. But I would not rule out the possibility that Gingrich could leap out of a pond and grab you by the leg. He's just so enthusiastic about his new ideas.

For one, Gingrich feels strongly that the U.S. is no longer a world leader because we've lost our global competitive edge. But then, he's probably never checked out youtube.com, the greatest example of productivity in American history. I'd like to see the Chinese come up with "Cute Puppy Falling Asleep," a video that I have personally watched more than a dozen times, never failing to get a lump in my throat for living in a country where a man can take a short six-hour break in the middle of the work day and watch "Hands Farting the Star Spangled Banner" or "Squirrel Playing Guitar." Clearly, these are labors of love from Americans who know a thing or two about creativity, especially the kind that's usually grainy and poorly lit.

GINGRICH ALSO WANTS to bring back fiduciary responsibility, by having a pay-as-you-go federal budget approach "just like the American people, who have to balance their budgets every month." Not to quibble on a small point, but Americans haven't balanced their budgets since credit cards were first mailed out in the 1960s. (My parents didn't know what to do with theirs, so I cut them up into guitar picks. Here's an idea: If more Americans used their credit cards to play music maybe we wouldn't have the lowest savings rate in the world.)

Other politicians have big ideas, too, though mainly just the one about being president. There's a growing list of Republican hopefuls that Gingrich—who is thinking of running on the Know-It-All platform—will have to contend with:

- Rudy Giuliani is the current front-runner for the Republican nomination, now that John McCain has flown too close to the sun and the popularity of his pro-war stance has begun to melt like Icarus, which is either a figure in ancient mythology or the latest General Motors line of unsellable cars. Now all that's left for Giuliani, who is pro-choice, pro-gay, and pro-gun control, is to prove he's actually a Republican.

- Kansas Sen. Sam Brownback is running on a Traditional American Values platform, also known as "Let's Go Back to the '50s," a magic time when men were men, and other people—like women, minorities, the poor—were not.

- And finally, former Massachusetts Gov. Mitt Romney is running on the "For and Against" gay marriage platform, since he can't seem to make up his mind. If elected, he would be our first Mormon president. Come to think of it, he'd also be our first president named "Mitt," which unfortunately does not have quite the gravitas of, say, a "Newt." ∎

Eighty in a 55 Zone

One of the greatest challenges of my generation is caring for our aging parents, now that medical advances are enabling them to use up our inheritance at a much faster rate. Not to mention how they selfishly spend Social Security money that could otherwise be given to needy defense contractors.

I was reminded of this when my own 80-year-old father and late-70s mom came for a visit and left me with a strong impression: 80 isn't 80 any more.

A long time ago, my great-grandfather was that age when my cousins and I would visit him in his one-room shack behind our grandparents' house. We would sit on rickety furniture in that darkened little space, four 8-year-old boys convinced that the unfamiliar odor of chewing tobacco could only be the smell of death. Great-Grandpa's hearing was mostly gone, so he spoke loudly, punctuating his reminiscences with periodic spits of tobacco juice into a nearby coffee can. Did I mention he was toothless and laughed with a high-pitched cackle? On average, we lasted about five minutes before we would flee, shaken by the ordeal, and take refuge in a nearby tree.

These days you seldom see the elderly with tobacco juice dribbling down their chins. (My own mother has gotten much better about this, especially when company comes over.) Now they whiz down the road with big plans and bigger cars, blowing the dust off unused shuffleboards as they speed by. My father still exudes brash self-confidence during a winter visit as he walks up to my front door, whips out a bundle of bills, and says, "Son, here's 50 bucks. Now turn up the heat."

To be sure, my parents are slowing down considerably. Because of his advanced age, my father has been reduced to playing a mere three rounds of golf per week. And his growing physical limitations have made him decide to stop doing his own roof repairs "in a few years." (Roof repair happens a lot in coastal Florida. Coincidentally, in another example of the stubbornness that can come with aging, my father refuses to believe that the Bush administration was responsible for an increased incidence of hurricanes. "OH SURE!" I reply testily, "Ignore the science!")

My dad's daily exercise regimen is also beginning to show evidence of age-related fatigue. He's finally at the point where I can almost bench-press as much as he does. Another hundred pounds, and I'm SO going to out-lift him!

Looking on the bright side, my brother and I have been waiting for decades to get the better of our dad in arm-wrestling. After years of humiliation at the dining room table, it looks like sometime in the next decade we'll be able to crow, "Take THAT, Mr. 90-year-old! NOW who's your Daddy!?" Of course, we'll taunt him from a discreet distance, so as to avoid our father's conciliatory handshake or loving embrace (known, respectively, as the Crushing Vice-Grip From Hell or the Knock-Your-Breath-Out Bear Hug of Pain, also From Hell.)

IT SEEMS MY DAD'S AGE has further hampered his mental judgment, given that he recently retired as head usher at church—a gig with obvious power and authority—preferring instead to be, ahem, the doorman of the nursery. When he could be schmoozing with his peers, he has inexplicably chosen to watch over young children waiting for parents after worship. I have seen these children, their faces downcast at leaving a man who'd just put a shiny new quarter in their little hands and who'd said goodbye in the unmistakable voice of Donald Duck. For the first time in their young lives, these children must face the fact that their own parents—who have never spoken to them in the voice of Duck—may become grave disappointments to them.

My mother, too, is beginning to show signs of aging. She has cut back significantly on her daily routine, and now only stays up a couple hours past midnight working on correspondence and computer research for the church library. I can relate to that schedule. When she finally goes to bed, I've already been asleep for hours, exhausted despite my youth from another evening of tea-making and page-turning.

Surprisingly, my parents have adopted a moderate attitude toward current events, even though their preferred information source is Fox Spews (sorry, Fox News). In fact, I'm more often the one throwing decorative pillows at the during political talk shows, uttering epithets that can only be described as, well, crotchety.

Be that as it may, my parents will continue to grow older and the day will come when I, as the oldest child, will need to take charge of their care. I accept this responsibility and have assured them that I will spare no effort, no expense, and no sacrifice when it finally comes time to move them in with my sister. ∎

So, How About That Economy?

March, 2007

While Congress debates President Bush's FY08 budget and tries to find the responsible middle ground between hopeless optimism and criminal self-delusion, economists are looking at the current fiscal crisis to determine whether the economy is:

a) at the beginning of a recession,

b) experiencing a mid-course correction, or

c) caught in a raging river of financial despair without a paddle, a life preserver or, for that matter, a Life Saver. (Not that fruit-flavored candy would help in a time like this, but I've found that eating a red one can turn a frown upside down. It's my Happy Color.)

Many of you are already convinced this country is in recession, given that you've lost your job, your home, or your savings. But I remind you that yours is merely anecdotal evidence of a downturn, and hardly germane to the broader economic conversation. You can't just up and use the "R" word without proper credentials. That's for the financial experts, who know what they're talking about—since they talk about it all the time on television. And, attractive people on television are *never* wrong.

According to these people—who, to their credit, actually

reside in at least one of the houses they own—a recession is only recognizable after it has ended. I mention this only to reassure you that, as hard as things are for you right now, you needn't worry. The experts will be just fine.

Because they're rich.

BUT THE REST OF US need to get our economic house in order (those who still have a house), cut back on expenses, roll up our sleeves (those who haven't sold their sleeves for food), and generally be more responsible with our spending.

Hahahaha! Just kidding. We couldn't possibly do those things! We don't know how. They didn't teach that stuff in school, although I can't be sure, since I nodded off most days after saying the Pledge of Allegiance. (I usually woke up again in health class, when they were showing driving safety films, which showed us that, according to experts on the behavior of young people, in life you have two choices: Live or drive.)

I personally have looked closely at my spending habits to find places to cut back. Unfortunately, all I could come up with was my nighttime cleansing ritual using a brand-name lotion. (It has Ultra Calming™ emollients.) Perhaps I could scrimp on favorite shampoo, but it contains volumizing ingredients for thinning hair which, in my opinion, is the greatest single invention in the past century (and yes, I'm counting penicillin. Infection or no infection, you want to look good on a Saturday night, right?) Either of these products could be called an indulgence, but I would quickly and forcefully defend each as a necessity. Because, after all, I'm worth it.

During a recession, however, it turns out I'm not worth it. So now I just use joint compound for both face and hair. It's cheap, and you get used to the smell.)

FORTUNATELY, such steps may become unnecessary, since our government has devised a plan to provide both jobs and money for struggling Americans. On the jobs side, the State Department has announced hundreds of immediate openings in its Baghdad embassy, no experience required. (THAT'll teach those career diplomats who refuse to go!) Yes, the jobs are in a war zone, and the new building has been plagued by faulty construction and declared unfit for occupancy. But if you can put two sentences together in Arabic—and maybe know how to hook up a toilet—you qualify. (Early-bird hiring bonus: Mail your résumé today and receive a list of which outlets you can use without fear of electrocution.)

On the money side, Congress is working on a stimulus package, which includes a rebate of as much as $600 per person. Spent wisely, this money could help grow the economy. And by wisely, I don't mean paying bills or putting it in savings. Please. How unpatriotic can you be? You need to buy things, new things, to get this economy up and running on empty again.

I'm thinking of spending my own rebate on a new futon because, scientists tell us, "it's a pillow for your whole body!" Unfortunately, the best ones are from Sweden, a nation whose economy doesn't need stimulating, what with universal health care, full employment, and a high quality of life. (But they don't live in formerly the richest and previously the most powerful nation on earth, do they?)

So maybe I'll buy a new sump pump instead. But not just any sump pump, a high-end BJM Submersible, with a cast-iron impeller that can empty a flooded basement before you can say "Honey, have you seen the cat?" It's like having a jet engine in your house: A little drainage problem and then WOOOSH, it's gone! (Manufacturer's Warning: May also expel loose garden tools, poorly installed ceiling tiles, and other unsecured objects.) ("Fluffy!")

On second thought, maybe I'll just go with the futon. After

laying on it for a while, I'll sink down so deep that I won't see the television, with its constant crawl of bad news. A couple more days and I won't be able to get up for the newspaper, either. "What recession?" I'll ask, as I lay in my comfortable cotton trough, separated from the outside world by cushiony, double-stitched walls. And if I need something to read, there's always the manufacturer's warning label: "Caution: May include industrial foam from China. Avoid contact with skin. Or pajamas.") ■

The Man Without a Face

R ecently, some spots on my face were diagnosed not as the distinctive markings of a rare intellect—which I had assumed them to be—but as a precancerous skin malady. In strict medical terms, the condition is known as "Having A Face That Looks Like Butter Pecan Ice Cream," and it needed to be treated right away.

Unfortunately, this required a visit to Dr. Bob's House of Pain. That's not what he calls his office, of course, but then his is a slightly different perspective than mine. I'm the guy on the table, on my back, wondering, "Hey, what's that burning smell?"

When the dermatologist first told me he'd have to cauterize the spots, I asked him if it would hurt. "It all depends on what you mean by 'hurt,'" he replied. I hadn't thought I was asking a complex question. But he went on to explain that people have different thresholds of pain: A higher threshold means you can put up with a greater degree of discomfort, such as reality shows on network television. A lower threshold means you reach the point of discomfort much earlier, like, in my case, on the drive over.

He sympathized with my state of nervous apprehension (which at that point, was more like a continent) and assured me that Novocain would help. This assurance lasted only as long as it took him to pull out a hypodermic needle the size of a tennis ball can. He would have to inject each of the nine skin spots, he calmly related.

"Will it hurt?" I asked.

"It all depends on what you mean by...."

Fine. Nine shots, or nine burns with a hot needle-like thingy. I kept waiting for the third option. (Slow lingering death? Okay, I'll take that one.) I helpfully pointed out that my dentist uses a desensitizing cream before injecting Novocain, but the doctor replied, "Oh, we don't do that here." "Where, exactly, *do* you do it?" I asked. "I'd be happy to change rooms." "Hah," he said.

The procedure only took a few minutes. Not normal minutes, of course. But some strange, new kind of minute. A minute that has a beginning and an end, but also this real long part in the middle, which, in my case, was spent praying that a police SWAT team would knock down the door and rescue me from this madman. I'M A HOSTAGE...AND I CAN'T GET UP!

That kind of minute.

It felt like someone putting out a cigarette on my forehead. Nine times. And after each one, Dr. Helpful would keep count: "That's one. Only eight more to go. That's two. Only seven more to go...." I never realized just how long it takes to get to the number nine.

But this is a humor piece, so let's get right to the funny part of the story. Let's see... People stared at me when I walked out of the hospital because I had huge welts on my forehead. No, that wasn't funny. Back at the office my colleagues tried to get my mind back on the important work at hand: "So Ed, I read your memo and WHAT HAPPENED TO YOUR FACE???!!!" No, that's not the funny part either.

Oh yeah [giggle], now I remember the funny part. It still hurt TWO HOURS LATER!

So let this be a warning to you. These skin spots were

caused by a lifetime of ill-advised exposure to th sun. When I was a young child in the 1950s there was no such thing as sunscreen, only the sun "tan" lotions that scientists later discovered worked better for cooking French fries.

Researchers now know that the best protection from the sun is called "the indoors." But if you do go out into the sun, just put on what I wear: two bedsheets, a sombrero, and a ski mask.

Or you could go to Dr. Bob. And ask him if it will hurt. ∎

Hollywood in the White House.
Again.

August, 2007

A t last count, there were 327 men competing for the Republican presidential nomination; far too many to name here, but ultimately of little consequence since none has a chance against one man who has quietly sat on the sidelines for most of this political dogfight. He calmly watched as the others snapped and snarled at each other, their furry coats slick with sweat, their claws bloody, their eyes crazed, their tongues hanging with exhaustion ....

Okay, enough with the dogfight analogies. Sorry. Sometimes these literary constructs take on a life of their own. We'll just press on and assume you can discuss politics without animal references, such as the fact that Newt Gingrich looks like a Chow Chow. (Hey, don't start Googling for pictures. Just trust me on this one.)

At a time when the Republicans have little to run on besides war, trillion-dollar deficits, and rising inequality—nothing that really stands out as a good bumper sticker—the one man who can hold the White House is Fred Thompson. The lawyer-turned-actor-turned-politician-turned-actor-again has recently declared his candidacy—although he has yet to explain all those hyphens—after spending several weeks in

Iowa keeping us "guessing." But let's not be jaded here. There are lots of reasons to visit Iowa, such as the dairy museum, which there's probably one of. Not to mention clean restrooms in various locations throughout the state.

Of all the potential nominees, Fred Thompson is the closest thing to Ronald Reagan that his party has seen in a generation. And he's got all the qualifications to be president:

- He's an actor.

In other words, he's ready to tackle the toughest issues in the way Americans most expect: by pretending to be strong. We want steely eyes of resolve, a determined jaw, broad shoulders, a towering physique, and an Actor's Equity card, none of which are possessed by other Republican hopefuls. Giuliani, a towering physique? Please. Newt Gingrich, steely eyes? Try beady. (Actually, a Chow Chow has beady eyes ... made you look.) John McCain, a determined jaw? Not since he gave the commencement grovel at Jerry Falwell's school, Red State University. Mitt Romney might qualify for the actor's union, but only because he looks like a game show host.

At 6 foot 3, Fred Thompson would make us proud in those summit photos by towering over other world leaders, most of whom are short and stooped, having spent much of their early lives at desks studying languages, science, and history. You know, the boring stuff. For Americans, it's not what you know, but how good you look when you're not knowing it.

FOR THE DEMOCRATS to win, they'll need an equally strong candidate from the land of make-believe. And that man is Tommy Lee Jones.

Thompson may be a TV star, but Jones is an Academy Award-winning movie star. He eats TV guys for lunch. (Really. With a sprig of cilantro.) In more than 60 films, Jones has shown physical and emotional attributes far surpassing Thompson's. In Men In Black Jones stood up to aliens. Big aliens. And I counted at least three times when he personally saved the entire planet. (To this day, I remain grateful.)

If Jones can stare down a six-story alien cockroach, you think he'll have any trouble with Kim Jong Il, a much smaller bug?

In The Fugitive, a falsely accused Harrison Ford desperately pleads his innocence to U.S. Marshal Tommy Lee Jones: "I didn't kill my wife!" Unmoved, Jones coldly replies, "I. Don't. Care." Osama bin Laden may have his reasons, but pity him if he tries to explain them to our President Jones.

I've got chills.

When President Jones stares into the eyes of Vladimir Putin, he may or may not get a sense of the soul George Bush claims to have seen. But Putin will definitely be standing in a puddle of his own making.

And let's be honest: Ronald Reagan only pretended to be a cowboy on his ranch—riding horses and clearing brush. Jones played a REAL cowboy in Lonesome Dove. (For the record, farmhands clear brush, not cowboys. Cowboys eat farmhands for lunch. Really. With a sprig of alfalfa.) And, unlike our current president, who was born in, ahem, Connecticut, Jones really is a Texan. He was born on the hot and dry side of Austin, which explains why his face looks like a drought hit it.

A campaign between Thompson and Jones won't be pretty. The Republicans will play dirty and reveal that Jones' first film role was in Love Story—I'll pause briefly while you shudder involuntarily—but who among us is not guilty of youthful indiscretions? Al Gore, please put your hand down.

And speaking of Al Gore, do you think Fred Thompson was *his* college roommate? Nope. Tommy Lee Jones: The next president of the United States. ■

Rites of Fall

Consider the ravens, for they neither sow nor reap.
And neither do they drive their daughter
back to college in the fall.
So I'm thinking the ravens got off easy.   —Luke 12:22ish RSVP

Like death and tax breaks for the rich, autumn brings its own inevitabilities: the crisp, clean air of coming winter, the rhythmic raking of fallen leaves, and the certainty that, at some point during the day, I will drop something really heavy on my foot.

It is time to take my oldest daughter—and all her stuff—back to school, a time of the year made bittersweet by the thought of losing a child (that's the bitter part, in case you were confused), but at the same time regaining a room—a room which can finally be returned to its rightful state of order, a shrine to neatness that one can actually walk into without stepping on a cell phone, or a partially eaten snack, or a cat in the process of eating that snack. This is a room we can now give tours of when friends come over (after which we move them quickly past our younger daughter's room, with the closed door and hastily made sign we put up that says "STORAGE"). With at least one of the children's rooms clean and quiet, I can finally stop wincing at the mental picture of a daughter—my own flesh and blood—hastily vacuuming around cell phones and food and then stopping to gaze proudly at her accomplishment. Set small goals, I always taught my girls, and then put them off for as long as you can.

As we packed the car—I say "we" with my usual mirthful irony—I dutifully made suggestions to scale back a little. I questioned, for example, the need for a second coffee pot, or the torn Josh Hartnett poster, or the complete Harry Potter series (in hardback). Not to mention the large clothes hamper which would be of no use since, by my observation, her dirty clothes are simply dropped directly onto the floor, presumably to protect the carpet from excessive wear. But my suggestions were met with heavy sighs of a child wise beyond (or well short of) her years.

Once loaded we drove off, heading toward the foothills of the Poconos. As always, the view out the front window was spectacular. Unfortunately, there were no views out the back or side windows, since these were obscured by carefully packed and sealed boxes which, at the last minute, were all opened and crammed with the stuffed animals that had been discovered hidden, parentally, in the closet. (I had to keep reminding myself that—despite what the rear view mirror was showing—we were not being pursued by a large brown ape with sad, twinkly eyes.)

THE GORGEOUS CAMPUS loomed above us as only the hills of Western New York can: lush, rolling, and—depending on how many clothes hangers were digging into my hands—very painful. The campus is built on a hill—a big hill—but the parking lots were conveniently placed at the bottom to distract the parent from the fact that, no matter how far he's driven, his journey is far from over. Whereupon groups of friendly Sherpas come up to the vehicles and begin negotiating a price. Actually, I made up the part about the Sherpas, and even if they were indigenous to New York, the Sherpas would probably look at my daughter's stuff, gaze up the hill to her dorm, and chuckle—Edmund Hillary-like—as they walked away.

So the trudges began, with predictable progress. My daughter would walk a few feet, then set down a box to squeal and embrace friends not seen since May. Meanwhile, I'm making five trips for every one of hers, and observing other fathers in similar straits. Sweating and groaning and looking for those worse off, we fathers silently evaluate each other: fathers of sons smirking at the dads carrying brightly colored plastic boxes of shoes, marked "DRESSY PARTY" and "CASUAL PAR-TY." (None, it seems, marked "LIBRARY" or "CLASS.") And the fathers of daughters shaking their heads in pity at dads dragging stereo speakers the size of dumpsters (speakers with suggestive brand names like "Anvil").

Meanwhile, their sons are caught up in their own intensely joyous reunions:

First guy: "Dude."

Second guy, agreeing: "Dude."

Third guy, with emotion: "Dudes."

And then we are finished, and I grow melancholy once more at the separation between father and daughter, and at the realization that in this, one of the nation's finest academic institutions, there's not one class on vacuuming. ∎

Oh Sure, Blame the Problem!

During a recent congressional hearing, Federal Reserve Chair Ben Bernanke blamed baby boomers for a looming fiscal crisis, declaring that future generations will be forced to "bear much of the cost" of Social Security and Medicare. Frankly, it's a mystery to me why future generations shouldn't be happy to pay for my anti-aging cream, but some people just insist on seeing the colander as half-empty.

Speaking as a member in good standing of the baby boom generation—as defined by my inability to listen to the Beach Boys' "Don't Worry Baby" without sobbing uncontrollably—I take offense at the idea that people my age are a "problem." After all, we have been called the Greatest Generation, for surviving the Depression through sheer force of pluck, for beating back totalitarianism in World War II, and then returning home to forge the largest economic expansion in the 20th century.

Oops. Sorry. That was my parent's generation. MY generation pretty much just laid around and watched TV. (But it was color TV! Sweet.) And as far as pluck goes, we didn't do pluck. Wouldn't know it if it hit us upside the head. No, what we did was cute and precious—also undeserving, ungrateful, and entitled, especially entitled, since our parents were determined that their children have all the things they never did. And who were we to argue?

They spoiled us with the most modern technological advances—such as Cool Whip—and did all they could to protect us from the hardships they had endured, such as growing up without Cool Whip. (And speaking of hardships, not to complain, but my allowance payments dropped off precipitously shortly after I turned 40. What's up with that?)

The point is, Mr. Bernanke, should my generation be looked down on just because our principal accomplishment is ... uhm ... that we are the greatest living depository of television trivia in the known world? Go ahead, ask me a question, any question, as long as it's about *Leave It To Beaver.* (The answer is: False. Eddie Haskell did not appear until the seventh episode.)

And that's not our only claim to fame. As children, we were the first in history to actually refuse food. Previous generations were grateful for any gruel-like substance placed in front of them, but not ours. I can still remember the day—a crisp October afternoon, a time when previous generations were proving themselves gruel-worthy by toting this and lifting that—and I was outside playing cowboys and mailman with my friends. (We all had cowboy clothes except this one kid, who liked to go house to house wearing a postal service uniform and ... well ... never mind.) My father whistled me in for dinner, and I arrived at the table to see something red on my plate. To my mother's credit, the unfamiliar object had been julienned decoratively, and was almost the exact color of my beloved cranberry sauce, harvested, I always suspected, already in the cans. I took one bite, experiencing what could only have been the cruel joke of a spiteful god.

Since that fateful day, I have been unrelenting in my antagonism against all members of the beet species, and recently launched a campaign to take these vile roots out of the mouths of unsuspecting children and put them where they can do the most good: namely, in our gas tanks. Yes, I'm talking about Beetanol, the key to ending our dependence on foreign oil, which you also shouldn't eat. Instead of using corn for fuel—cornanol, I think it's called—when corn is a staple of many countries, why not use something that, as far as I can tell, almost nobody eats? What, you think there'd be massive beet riots in developing countries? Would the streets run red—as riot police stood imposingly nearby—with beat juice? I don't think so.

But, I digress.

"THE LONGER WE WAIT, the more severe, the more draconian the adjustments are going to be," Bernanke continued in his testimony, though what Dracula has to do with it I don't know. (Editors' note: Actually, "draconian" comes from the name "Draco," an Athenian law scribe who insisted that small offenses deserved heavy punishments. Modern-day examples would be long prison sentences for minor drug violations, or having to endure Katie Couric in your own home just because you innocently turned on the television at 6:30 Eastern, 5:30 Central.)

(Wait, here's another one: How about getting hit by a car when your only crime was to cross the street while talking on your cell phone and listening to your iPod? Now THAT'S draconian. PLEASE, people! Future civilizations are going to discover the skeletal remains of humans lying on ancient streets, and wonder if we were killed by the venomous bites of giant cicada-like objects attached to the sides of our heads. I'm just sayin' ....)

But we should heed Mr. Bernanke's warning, and be grateful for wisdom from any of the Bush administration's many independently wealthy officials. Yes, my generation should not rest on its laurel, once it finds that laurel. I personally have set an important goal for the coming years: I hope eventually to complete one of those Sudoku puzzles in less than the full week it usually takes me. It looks easy, but those numbers make it hard to write in the crosswords. It's just part of the challenge, I guess. ∎

No Visible Means of Support

As a father who has raised two children successfully (judged by the fact they seldom drool), I feel qualified to observe and comment on today's version of *familius americanis typicalis*. To put this in perspective, let's first review a moment from 1990, when two young parents were attempting to establish good nutritional standards for their youngsters.

Wife: Eat your steamed carrots, please.

Daughter #1: Okay, Mom.

Daughter #2: All gone, Mommie.

Husband: But...they're yucky.

Many years have passed for this control family, and the children have reached adulthood with a clear sense of self and vocation, although somewhat divided in the important category of church preference. While the oldest, like her mother, considers herself Catholic, the youngest does not. Thus, she and her father—a recovering Southern Baptist—feel the need to wear Groucho Marx glasses when taking communion. They also hope no one asks them for the secret handshake.

Religious issues aside, however, I understand the challenges facing today's young parents. When I see them in public places, I often walk up and helpfully shout out important suggestions, such as "Why are you just standing there?! You should be home saving for college!" They look at me, their eyes wide with deep appreciation, and I walk away happy to have touched another life.

And I'm especially concerned about the bewildering array of devices new parents feel compelled to use with their youngsters. Take the modern child carrier, for example. Gone are the days of carrying your child in a backpack where she was free to enjoy the view, lovingly pick at her dad's baldspot, and reach around to grab his eyeglasses and fling them under a passing bus. Instead, today's child is strapped to the parent's chest, face forward, with legs dangling and arms flailing.

In these front carriers, the child feels alone, suspended in mid-air with no visible means of support, floating above sidewalks and wondering if he's being used as an emergency flotation device. (Child to parent: "What am I, your airbag?!")

At best, the child thinks the shoes walking in and out of view far below are his own, and that he's really, really tall. At worst, however, we're raising an entire generation of children who think they can fly.

One wonders what will happen when, say, on the first day of kindergarten a child shows up with the bold self-confidence you get when you're a 4-year-old with super powers. (Child: "Hey, now that I finally got rid of that dead weight on my back, watch how high I can fly!" Teacher: "Carl, it's circle time. Please come down off the bookcase.")

And have you seen the play seats they put babies in these days? A recent visit to our 4-month-old niece found her sitting in a large circular device with at least a dozen dials, wheels, and gizmos. My own children sat in a simple wheeled chair, which permitted them to roll around and experience the mysteries of their home environment, such as what cat hair tastes like. But today's child is trapped in a device that looks like the cockpit of a space shuttle. And just as complicated, even for an extremely intelligent adult like me. I tried unsuccessfully to manipulate this one object until finally the baby reached out, moved it a quarter turn to the left, and up popped a smiley clown singing a little jingle. (In my defense, the baby had read the instruction manual.) Anyway, an hour alone in this over-stimulating device and a kid needs a cigarette just to calm down.

And don't get me started about those blinking tennis shoes. Are they designed for these kids to lead their parents into darkened tunnels and caves? (And if so...is it a trap?!) On dark nights, do airline pilots get confused while landing and follow the rows of lights into Chuck E. Cheese's or a Toys R Us?

THE GOOD NEWS is that today's kids are made of strong stuff. Recently I drew the short straw to take my young nephew outside to play. It was in Cleveland and it was winter (or is that redundant?), and the frigid northern Ohio winds whipped unceasingly up my sleeves and down my neck. The 2-year-old didn't seem to notice, though, because he was poking a piece of ice with a stick. For an hour.

I was so numb from the cold I declined the child's invitation to get my own stick and join in the fun. Fortunately, a passing St. Bernard saw the blinking lights and rescued me. ∎

There's Something in the Room

November, 2007

(Editor's note: This piece was written during the early primary process for the 2008 presidential election and includes the suggestion that gorillas be used for consensus-decision making in Congress. Actually, they've decided to use pit bulls, a breed more genetically compatible with elected representatives, and not just because Fred Thompson looks like one.)

Reporter: As the primary season progresses and the inevitable wreckage shows up on the side of the road—Gilmore who? What's a "biden"?—it is fascinating that Republican Rudy Giuliani is still in the lead for his party's nomination. Despite being pro-choice, pro-gun control, and pro-gay marriage, positions that go against fundamental GOP tenets, Giuliani is the 800-pound gorilla in a crowded field of dogmatic loyalists.

800-Pound Gorilla: Ahem.

Reporter: Oh, sorry. I didn't see you standing there.

Gorilla: People always say that.

Reporter: So, you're, like, Koko, or what?

Gorilla: [sigh] No, my name is Robert. Koko's that idiot who thinks he can type. Like that's hard. And that so-called "sign language" he uses? You'd make those gestures, too, if you had a piece of dung beetle larvae on your finger. (Actually, they're quite tasty after a good rain, but you don't want to get that stuff on your keyboard.)

Reporter: If you'll excuse me, we're talking about presidential politics. Fred Thompson is another force to reckon with. Despite his advanced age and minimal public service, compared to most other candidates he's another...uhm...

Gorilla: You were going to say "800-pound gorilla" again, weren't you?

Reporter: Was not.

Gorilla: Look, these constant references to my specis are very annoying. While part of me is flattered that I'm used as a reference for something substantial and imposing, the other part of me is ...

Reporter: Really hairy?

Gorilla:

Reporter: Sorry.

Gorilla: My point is, I am not just a symbol of overwhelming power. I have a sensitive side that's never talked about. An 800-pound gorilla could lend a certain dignity to any proceeding, even the most contentious gathering. On Capitol Hill, for example, I could easily bring an end to partisan bickering with a simple nudge from one of my huge, fleshy hands, or perhaps with an unyielding stare from my deep-set yellow eyes. Or I could just squash their heads.

Reporter: I see.

Gorilla: Having a huge bull ape in the room could enforce a respectful discourse that only comes when opposing parties know that, at any moment, they could be flung against a wall with brute force. It's a role to which I would gladly give my full attention, except for those occasional moments of personal grooming, which may or may not include popping a large tick in my mouth.

Reporter: But—and I'm not sure how to say this delicately—you're naked.

Gorilla: On the contrary, my body is completely covered by a thick and lustrous coat. It's not like I'm one of those godawful baboons who parade around with their obscenely naked red butts. They might as well be carrying a billboard that says, "Hey LOOK AT MY OBSCENELY NAKED RED BUTT!",

Reporter:

Gorilla: Sorry. I had a bad baboon experience in my youth. And I'd rather not talk about it.

Reporter: Ooooo-kay. So anyway, do you think we should go back to the tried-and-true phrase "elephant in the room"?

Gorilla: Possibly. Elephants are grand and docile behemoths which, when domesticated, often work side by side with their human partners.

Reporter: How would you know that?

Gorilla: I saw it on a National Geographic special.

Reporter: By the way, no offense, but have you ever thought about cutting back on the carbs a little, and maybe being a 700-pound gorilla? I'm just sayin' ...

Gorilla: You're right. I've tried to go easy on the bananas, but they're not as filling as you might think. I start out wanting to eat just one—the potassium is an important nutritional component for the bull ape on the go—but they have almost no fiber, but before you know I look down and the forest floor is littered with yellow peels. Ook.

Reporter: Did you just say "ook"?

Gorilla: Yes. It's a word my species uses to express guilt after a regretful self-indulgence. Like reading this, for example.

Reporter: Ook. ∎

The Name is "Maestro"

There comes a time in a man's life when he needs to take on new challenges, to stretch himself, to spread his wings, even though, if history is any guide, they will be wings of mediocrity. As one who proudly uses the term "above average" in his résumé, who becomes swollen with misplaced pride after accomplishing the simplest of tasks, such as flossing, I nonetheless wanted to try something completely different. Plus, there was nothing good on TV.

For a middle-aged man looking for new pursuits, the choices are unlimited. The interests of my youth were still tempting, of course, but I didn't want to settle too quickly on becoming a cowboy or astronaut. Nuclear science sounded like a good hobby, but it would probably require some remedial study. Likewise, weekend fishmonger carries a certain cachet, what with the cool rubber apron. But in the end, I settled on learning the violin.

How hard could it be? Several of my friends have young children who take lessons, and they don't have half the life skills I could apply to learning the instrument. (I'm an excellent typist, for example, giving me the dexterity one needs to play in, like, the New York Philharmonica, or whatever.) Plus, attending weekly beginners classes with 5- to 8-year-olds would mean that, finally, I'd be the big kid in school. (Oh, yes ... it's payback time.) Unfortunately, a person my age is not welcome in that class, so my mother won't know the joy of attending a concert and whispering to a friend, "That's my son, the tall one in the back."

So I settled for a private teacher, a respected soloist who was a child prodigy at age 12 and, unlike most prodigies, grew up to be the size of an offensive lineman. This is definitely NOT a guy whose motorcycle you want to mess with, if he has one, which he doesn't, although he looks like he does.

Turns out, he's also a licensed dog rescuer. So when I waited for my first lesson in his living room, several large animals surrounded me, drooling and nudging me to find a meaty part to chew on. Dog breath notwithstanding, the hardest part of waiting was listening to a beautiful Beethoven interpretation coming from the other room—and then watching as a teenager walks out, chewing her gum in a superior manner. (You know how violinists can get. I hear Itzhak Perlman gives noogies to lesser musicians when he passes by.)

Then it was my turn. I walked in with my rented violin and confidently assured the teacher that I should have no trouble learning the instrument, just as soon as the pit bull lets go of my leg. ("Peanut, put him down!") Peanut? Impressed at my self-confidence, he immediately assigned me a difficult classical piece by Mozart. (You didn't know that "Twinkle, Twinkle, Little Star" was by Mozart, did you?)

IT HAS BEEN SAID that the violin is the only instrument that can replicate the complexity of the human voice or, in my case, the voice of a human that just slammed his fingers in the car door. Frankly, I was surprised at the difficulty of learning the instrument, despite the rigorous discipline of playing several minutes each day. My failure to master the violin has left me with only one conclusion: There is a fundamental design flaw in the instrument.

For one thing, the violin doesn't come with a strap, so you have to—get this—actually hold it against your neck. I kid you not. Like you're changing a pillow case or something. Plus, it gives you a double chin, and at my age who needs that?

The finger board of the violin contains no frets, thus permitting endless variations for a single note, all but one of which is terribly, painfully, wrong. Either you play the note precisely right, or the cats walk around with a migraine and small cracks appear in your home's foundation.

And then there's the bow. What, all that creativity during the Renaissance and they couldn't invent the guitar pick? (And just try to play the violin under a low-hanging ceiling fan. Trust me, you only do that once.)

On the other hand, the bow is useful for pointing out unwashed dishes in the sink and for scratching your back after a shower. And it's great for poking cats to get off things.

As hard as it is to play, at least the violin looks good around the house. It's kind of artistic, resting on the antique cabinet in the dining room, like one of those Cézanne still lifes: You know, Violin With Wild Flowers and Wild Game, perhaps. Or, in my case, Violin With Unfolded Laundry and Remote Control. (So THAT'S where it is!)

BUT, UNDAUNTED, I will continue to practice for the day that I can provide musical gravitas to our office worship services. I can already imagine the grateful wincing of joy in the faces of the congregation, with every head bowed and every hair reverently standing on end. And I just thought of something: "Twinkle, Twinkle, Little Star" is sort of an Advent song, right? ∎

Nor'easters for Peace

December, 2007

Editors' Note: It was the winter of 2007 in the nation's capital. Once again the author found himself with a few thousand Americans—whose cable television signal had apparently shut down—who gathered to protest the continuation of the Iraq War. It was one of those blinding winter storms that make the three meteorologists who coincidentally happen to be employed by Exxon-Mobil to stand up together and say "See. We TOLD you there's no such thing as global warming.!)

F illed with the Holy Spirit—who had already performed the miracle of ending a worship service on time, despite the participation of more than a dozen major religious leaders (you know how they can talk)—we walked out of the Washington National Cathedral and into the path of a blinding winter storm that I would have described as cold and bitter, had I been able to make my mouth work.

At this point, instead of marching to the White House, I felt God was calling us to march someplace closer, such as a nearby coffee shop, where we could get something hot. ("Could I get 3,000 regular grandes to go, please, and one espresso mocha skim latte with two vanilla shots. That one is for a major religious leader.") But before I could share this divine revelation, the marchers had embarked on the three-and-a-half mile walk to the home of the president, despite the fact that the vice president's house was only a couple blocks away. (And he had coffee.) I tried to mention this, but I was swept up by the surge.

Speaking of the vice president, I finally understood what he meant when he patiently explained he wasn't lacking in patriotism when he avoided the draft during the Vietnam War. He just had "other priorities." I felt the same way when I decided not to join a couple hundred of my friends this evening who were getting arrested at the White House. Having been jailed several times for acts of civil disobedience, I felt my solidarity was better expressed in my prayerful support. So as we marched I kept a keen eye out for a diner with a large window where I could sit and express that support, mainly by waving, prayerfully.

But on we walked, thousands strong, and I felt if we wanted to we could just SHUT DOWN THIS TOWN, BABY! Well, maybe just a few blocks, but we would SO OWN THOSE BLOCKS! At this point, a colleague (Jack, who will remain nameless) came up to me and said with a mocking laugh, "You look like a Russian peasant woman." Instead of pointing out the insulating advantages of multiple layers—not to mention the good sense of the Soviet Bloc women to whom he alluded—I chose a more direct and slightly less-Christian remark about his stupid-looking hat. Then, as if sin carries its own immediate punishment, I stepped in a hole filled with water.

This was the first of a series of potholes I would step in during the march, which I thought I had prepared for by wearing brand-name storage bags over my socks. After the third hole I recalled that the box had no warning against using the product for winter peace marches. This will no doubt be corrected once they receive my letter.

In this march we were trying to send a message of peace to George Bush, a man that many analysts say is the worst president in the last century, and maybe even in this century, although it's too early to tell. Newt Gingrich could give him a run for his money, since he's gotten an early endorsement from conservative power-broker James Dobson. (Dobson is currently deciding which thrice-divorced non-Mormon best represents American family values.)

George Bush has failed despite the fact that, as president, he only has one job: to protect the Constitution. This should be easy, since the Constitution is already well-protected down-town at the National Archives. It's behind thick glass in this big metal case and there are all these guards standing around looking like they'd just love to break the monotony over your head. (For some reason, the Magna Carta is also there, al-though it's not, technically, an American document. I think it's there mainly to show school kids the actual thing that they got wrong on their world history test. Maybe now they'll remem-ber.)

Anyway, we PUSHED on, empowered by a Constitution that gives us the right to assemble and speak out freely against, in this case, winter. We marched emboldened by our convictions against the war, and inspired by the words and witness of Je-sus the Peacemaker who, it must be admitted, lived in a more reasonable climate. ∎

To the Blogosphere...and Beyond

A number of people have approached me and asked if I am going to start my own blog. Setting aside for the moment how they were able to approach me—since I keep furniture piled against my office door and, as a back-up deterrent, enjoy a morning sardines snack which creates sort of a force field against unsolicited proximity—their question gave me pause. After all, many of my colleagues already have their own blogs and post daily thoughts and reflections for the public-at-large or, in most cases, at-small. One excited co-worker recently rushed up to me and exclaimed, "I got 20 hits on my blog yesterday!" Since he showed no signs of physical injury, I presumed this meant 20 people had accidentally stumbled upon his blog and, seeing no pop-up ads to hold their interest, moved on to the more typical tasks for which the Internet was designed, such as shopping for discount flip-flops. (Did you know they make them for prom now?) I quickly moved past him, however, not wanting to encourage a type of "hall-blogging" that I fear could become an unwanted extension of the online version.

I've been observing this phenomenon for a while, watching as blogs have become a part of the "marketplace of ideas" that Oliver Wendell Holmes first mentioned in his classic detective novel The Case of the Tedious Typist Who Wouldn't Stop, Not for Anything. (Or maybe that was Sherlock Conan Doyle.)

What I have learned is that blogs—an acronym for Blowing Off Goals—are basically personal diaries that are open to the public. They are places to bare your soul and, depending on the size of your server, photos of you and your soul on vacation. Unfortunately, because of their preponderance on the Web, they clog up my Google searches for flip-flops. On the plus side, however, their relative obscurity makes them unattractive to advertisers, so blogs seldom display pictures of large infected toenails. This is a good thing. (I don't care HOW effective Dermasil is when used as directed; nobody needs to see that.)

I'VE OFTEN WONDERED why people would post their random musings on the Internet when they could just as easily prattle on to strangers at a bus stop. This always works for me. Why do I need people across the globe weighing in on my opinions when people waiting for the H4 do it every day? And with extra jostling for emphasis.

Blogs appear to be the natural outgrowth of our insatiable desire to be heard, to be recognized, to say, simply, "I exist [closed quote, parenthesis, colon, smiley face]. It's one of the things that separates us from the animals, although not the animals on You Tube, who are a species more advanced than our own. Otherwise, how could that cockatiel play golf?

Bloggers probably began as those children who meticulously transcribed their days' events into diaries, carefully locking them afterward with those little keys that, for reasons of genetic predisposition, they always hid in their sock drawer, which is absolutely the first place parents look. (Not that I would ever do such a thing, since you can open them with just a paper clip. So I've heard.)

As adults, these diarists found a new mechanism for their self-expression: the Annual Christmas Letter, the perfect medium to recount their perfect lives and that of their perfect children, this year featuring their perfect [name of exotic locale] vacation. But these letters are sent only once a year, an unacceptable limitation to people who feel their relatives need frequent updates on The Good Life They're Missing. The limitless capacity of the Internet was what they've been waiting for. That they now include their political and cultural views only intensifies my wish for them to experience Old Testament retribution, such as plagues, locusts, and high interest rates.

SO WHERE DOES THAT leave us? That depends on what we were talking about. Blogs, I think.

In an effort to test the ubiquitousness (sp?) [gesundheit] of blogs, I randomly created and then Googled awkward combinations of words and nonetheless found entries on "horse construction," "tofu cars," and "absurd lettuce." Additional investigation revealed there are more blogs about "picking your nose in public" than there are for "peace in our time."

If the popularity of blogs continues, will they eventually work their way down the cultural ladder to the primal level of, say, playground taunts? ("Hey, my dad gets more hits than your dad!") Will blogging ultimately jeopardize the very fabric of our society, drawing in even first-responders who would otherwise be protecting us? ("Four-alarm fire downtown!" "I'm on it, just as soon as I type in a few more thoughts on absurd lettuce.")

As the work force succumbs to incessant blogging, will this be the end of productive society as we know it? Will other nations take economic advantage of us as we sit, typing mindlessly about our day's minutiae?

That's the $64,000 question. Actually, adjusted for inflation, it's the $356,389.35 question.

Or one Euro. (I wonder if the Treasury Department has a blog?) ∎

Bring Them Home Now

January, 2008

As the Iraq war moves toward its fifth anniversary (which gift experts say should be commemorated with keepsakes of wood or, for the more modern couple, silverware), a weary nation is crying out with one voice: It's time to bring our contractors home.

Yes, it's time to hang out yellow ribbons for Blackwater, to cover our cars with bumper stickers that support the mercenaries, to wear with pride the red, white, and blue wristbands that say, simply, "You're either FOR our soldiers of fortune or for the terrorists."

Let's be honest here. Since the war began, it's been the contractors who've borne the true risks of bringing democracy to the people of Iraq. While U.S. soldiers perform their missions in full battle gear and armored vehicles, contractors do their duty with only sunglasses and a nasty attitude. They rarely use their weapons, except in extreme cases, such as when they're held up in traffic. And who can blame them? During rush hour, who among us hasn't wished we could spray a clogged intersection with sustained fire from automatic weapons? (If ever there was a justification for driving a Humvee bristling with AK47s, it's when you're late getting home to watch Oprah.)

Unfortunately for Blackwater, its employees have gotten

some bad press lately, mainly because they look like former members of the World Wrestling Federation, where the key job skills involve breaking chairs over each other's heads. (Admittedly, these were fake chairs, but the bravado was very real.) No question, these men are a little rough around the edges, but what better place to put them to work than in a foreign country desperate for the benefits of democracy and the free market system. And without capitalism, "freedom is just another word for nothin' left to bill for."

Chorus:
"You know, billin' was good enough for me,
good enough for me and other war profiteers,
such as Lockheed Martin."

I know. They don't write folks songs like they used to.

BEFORE THE WAR, Blackwater was a small North Carolina company providing security guards to the night shift at the local Piggly Wiggly. Now it's a billion-dollar international security firm with a bold new plan to privatize the military in times of war and—worst-case scenario—peace. In which case Blackwater plans to contracts its services to local law enforcement. Which means that some day you could be pulled over by two big guys in an unmarked van and charged with "driving while under the impression" that you lived in a free society. Then they'll break a chair over your head.

In fairness to Blackwater, its employees lack marketable skills for many mainstream vocations. Most are retired military, often from the Special Forces, which are trained to "own the night," to kill quickly, silently, and with impunity. It's hard to find a job like that in your hometown.

Oh, sure, they could work for an HMO, denying coverage for medical care. Who's going to argue with a guy turning the pages of your medical records with the point of a ninja knife?

Bill collection is another possibility, for obvious reasons. ("Pay up now and I'll give you back your arm.") But dental hygienist might be a stretch. "You could floss, or you could not floss. It's your choice, maggot."

Nope, the best employment option for these ex-soldiers is in the mercenary forces, which in earlier times often meant the French Foreign Legion, a destination of choice for troubled men angry about life and unlucky in love. Because nothing eases the pain of a broken heart like propping up petty dictators or corrupt businessmen. Or, in the case of Iraq, both.

Which brings us back to Blackwater, a company named for the ideal condition for undersea combat missions: water so dark a soldier is invisible to the enemy. Either that or they named it after the catchy Doobie Brothers ballad. You remember, "Mississippi moon won't you keep on shinin' on me ...."

Okay, maybe not.

IN RECENT hearings, Blackwater founder and former Navy Seal Erik Prince gave a calm and reasoned response to congressional nitpicking about Iraqi "innocent" bystanders, who, through no fault of Blackwater, always seem to be in the wrong place at the wrong time. Prince's basic point was that his company executes its mission within the legal limits allowable for a major Republican contributor. Not to put my spin on it.

Be that as it may, the hard question remains: Should we bring home the contractors now and risk leaving Iraq in chaos? Or do we keep them there for the foreseeable future, to help manage the chaos, particularly at busy intersections, until Iraqis are able to choose their own path? (Tip for Iraqis: When choosing your own path, try not to look suspicious, or make any sudden moves.) ∎

CODE BLUE! (Or is it red?)

M y heart has a curious sense of humor. Every three
or four years something strikes it as funny and it
chuckles arrhythmically in my chest. Maybe it's anticipating how humorous I look when, immediately thereafter,
I fall to the floor and come to rest with my face pressed against
the carpet. At that moment I usually think two things:

- I'm having a heart attack.

- This floor really needs vacuuming.

And then, of course, there's the ride in the ambulance with
the cool flashing lights and the neat siren. By the time I arrive at the hospital, I'm actually feeling much better and don't
see why I should stay. But then they do an electrocardiogram
(KGB) which shows an abnormal heart beat. I have to take the
doctor's word for this, since the print-out just shows a bunch
of squiggly little lines. Sort of like the artwork our kids used to
make and then we'd have to say what a fine job they did even
though it was just a bunch of squiggly little lines. (Sorry kids.
But I can't live with the lies any longer.)

So for the next three hours I'm walking around the emergency room with all these wires coming out of me, not realizing that my movements were sending false signals that I was
either having a major cardiac event or was standing in a pool
of water being struck repeatedly by lightning. This caused

nurses to come running. "SIR! You can't walk around here like that! Now please get back into your bed!"

"But I'm not tired. And, by the way, it's NOT a bed, it's a gurney. And why do they call it a gurney, anyway?"

Nobody ever answered that question, or the other interesting questions I had, except once when I asked, "What's this handle thingie do?"

"It turns off that man's oxygen, sir, and YOU SHOULD NOT BE TOUCHING STUFF! NOW GET BACK IN YOUR BED!!"

"You mean my gurney?"

"WHATEVER!"

It went like this for several hours, until they finally got around to drawing a quart of blood from my arm. They did this, I believe, to make me weak so I'd stay on the gurney. But they claimed it was for enzyme tests, the same tests given to Vice President Dick Cheney (the man who's just a heartbeat away from not being the vice president). In fairness to the nurses drawing my blood, they were sensitive to my squeamishness about such things, so they only left the big clear vials of bright red blood on my pillow RIGHT NEXT TO MY FACE just long enough for me to pass out.

The good news was that my doctors quickly diagnosed what was wrong with me: Either I'd had a heart attack, or hadn't had a heart attack. Or I'd eaten too many M&Ms at the office party earlier in the day. (It's hard to stop after just one bowl.) So they decided to admit me for more tests, which meant that I was sent upstairs to a room with an actual bed where I could finally get away from the constant noise of the ER and settle in to the constant interruptions of floor nurses.

I didn't sleep much, mainly because of the guy next to me who, judging by his steady moose-like snore, was getting plenty of sleep. At least until he was awakened abruptly at 5 in the morning when the following actual dialogue took place (reprinted here verbatim, which is a Greek word meaning "you really should have been there"):

Nurse (hurriedly): Wake up, sir. It's time to take you down to surgery.

Patient (groggily): Surgery?

Nurse: Yes, sir. Now stand up and remove your underwear.

Patient: Underwear?

Nurse: Yes. And we're on a pretty tight schedule.

Patient: Schedule?

Nurse (looking down at her clipboard): Is this room 3310?

Me (tired of this guy answering everything with a question): No. This is room 3312.

Nurse: Oh. Sorry.

Now THAT'S why I have such confidence in this country's health care system. It's the very BEST in the world. Unless you're sick.

"Sick?"

Oh, be quiet.

(Editor's Note: The author did not have a heart attack. He was released on his own recognizance a few hours later. Which was a good thing, because after he left a nurse came in and wondered if he'd already been taken to surgery.) ∎

One Man, One Clip

June, 2008

(Editor's note: This piece was written before the Supreme Court declared D.C.'s gun ban unconstitutional. Not to brag, but the author TOTALLY called it.)

As you read this, the U.S. Supreme Court is in its final stages of pretending to carefully consider the constitutionality of Washington, D.C.'s ban on handguns. The oral arguments in March hinted at the final decision, given that, while questioning counsel, Justice Antonin Scalia was also cleaning his Glock 9mm automatic and at one point sent his clerk out to get more bore oil. (Without frequent oiling—and I don't have to tell you this—burned powder can build up and foul the muzzle.)

Any day now the high court could hand down its decision, which most legal experts predict will overturn the gun ban, thus validating the National Rifle Association's long-held belief that, when crafting the Second Amendment, the founders made a clerical error by using the word "militias" instead of "any bunch of fun-loving guys with a few beers and a machine gun."

On the other hand, there is a chance that D.C.'s 32-year-old gun ban will stand, a ruling the court would announce by releasing dozens of flying monkeys—each wearing a decorative fez hat—into the skies above our city. Although this seems far-fetched (the ruling, not the monkey part).

For what it's worth, most Supreme Court justices do not live in the District of Columbia, preferring the suburban security of nearby pro-gun states Maryland and Virginia (motto: "I know what you're thinking. 'Did he fire six shots or only five?' Well, to tell you the truth, in all this excitement I kind of lost track myself. But being that this is a .44 Magnum, the most powerful handgun in the world, and would blow your head clean off, you've got to ask yourself one question: Do I feel lucky? Well, do ya, punk?")

Having no vote in Congress and thus unaccustomed to the full benefits of that whachacallit "democracy" thingie, D.C. residents had nonetheless hoped the majority will of our citizens would prevail. Although the court is mainly concerned about an individual's right to have a gun for self-protection, logic—not to mention facts, statistics, and ambulances that have to be hosed out every night—refutes this. Handguns are, in fact, used primarily in crimes of passion against family members, in deadly force against individuals and police officers, and in acts of suicide. Apprised of these truths by counsel for the District—which, by the way, has one of the lowest suicide rates in the country—the majority of justices replied by quoting a favorite axiom of Vice President Dick Cheney: "So?"

(Cheney made this statement when reminded that the majority of Americans oppose the war in Iraq. He also added, off the record, "... bunch of morons.")

In telegraphing their views, the conservative members of the court appeared to cling to the argument that guns are particularly necessary against criminal home invasion, a fearful event on anyone's list of things they don't want to happen, such as more air time for Ryan Seacrest. Granted, a handgun is a powerful negotiating tool with unexpected intruders, and it quickly compensates for the Disney-themed pajamas in which a homeowner would confront them. But home invasion almost never happens—it is statistically far less likely than a lottery win—compared to the proven societal negatives of a citizenry bristling with handguns.

Our only hope is the "reasonable regulation" that the court agreed could be applied to gun ownership, which means the District government can make people jump through hoops to qualify. And I'm hoping they'll be actual hoops, maybe flaming ones, with crocodiles on one side and a poison ivy patch on the other. And, when jumping through, you'd have to be barefoot and wear a funny hat, and one of those red clown noses. While singing your ABCs, backwards. At the DMV.

BUT PERHAPS WE should face the inevitable, set aside our prejudices, and start enjoying the many benefits of handgun ownership, such as streamlining consensus decision-making and expediting slow-moving service providers. For example, fast food gets a lot faster when you walk up to the drive-through window and say, with quiet dignity, "I don't have a car, but I've got a gun, and I don't want to see one pickle—not a single one—on my Cheesy Bacon Wrap. Understand?" Customer service is bound to improve.

The hardest part will be choosing which particular handgun to keep loaded and cocked at your bedside and, when venturing out, what type of holster will best convey your self-protection spirit. There's the low-slung design, which combines Western styling with fast-draw utility, but can cause chafing. Or you might prefer the more comfortable waist-high position, which tends to bind when sitting in those overstuffed chairs at Starbucks. And which style is best for running and firing wildly during a citizen's arrest? Important questions, since with all those new firearms out there, the city will definitely need more gun nuts to take the law into their own hands and help protect us. It's what the founders would have wanted. ∎

The Gospel of GREAT News!

How was your Christmas? Did you experience God's endless bounty in this, the greatest nation in the world? Did you gather around the tree in the morning and open all the gifts that Jesus had brought the night before, landing on the rooftop with his eight tiny disciples (or was it 12?), and squeezing down the chimney with his bag of brand-name products made at the North Pole, or at the very least, northern China?

Or am I thinking of Santa Claus? You know, the mythical figure based on Nicholas of Myra, a man of considerable inherited wealth who gave money to the needy. Not much is known of him, except that he probably did not dress in red, did not have cheeks like roses and a nose like a cherry, nor did he have a little round belly that shook when he laughed like a bowlful of jelly. These attributes are what marketing people call "value added" characteristics when something—or someone—is in drastic need of an update.

Take Jesus, for example. As far as we know Jesus went around almost barefoot, a little thin, and spent a lot of time with poor people. I mean, please. Doesn't sound like Son of God material to me. That's why, in this season of getting, it might be better to look at a gospel message that's more appropriate for our current cultural context.

I refer to the new, and much improved, Prosperity Gospel. It's the New Testament with a modern makeover, and it's spreading like wildfire. (Oops. Sorry, California. Sore subject. How about ... um ... selling like hotcakes?)

And who better to explain this new phenomenon than Dr. Norman Robertson—or, if you prefer his formal title, norman-robertson.com—the best-selling author and renowned speaker who thinks that Christians should be rich and, judging by the pinstripe suit and flashy tie in his promotional photos, he practices what he preaches.

For the past 20 years, Robertson has been using his books, CDs, and lectures to debunk what he calls the myth of the "poor Jesus." You know that one: the babe of low estate, born in a manger, wrapped in swaddling clothes, and, let's be honest, he didn't dress much better when he got older. Not really the kind of role model you want for today's fashion-conscious Christians. Robertson claims that scripture itself challenges our assumptions of Jesus' humble beginnings.

In Matthew 2:11, Robertson points out, regional monarchs bestowed expensive gifts on the baby Jesus. Frankincense, myrrh, and the Santa Maria, I think, all on the lavish end of the gift spectrum that today could only be found in the Neiman Marcus catalog. Of course, Dr. Robertson makes no mention of what the shepherds brought as tokens of their esteem, presumably a more modest gift, like maybe diaper service for a month; much more practical than frankincense, an aromatic resin whose subtle fragrance would get totally lost in your typical stable environment. (Regardless of what the song says, lowing is not the only thing the cattle do after a big meal.)

Robertson also cites Matthew 27:35—which tells of soldiers casting lots for Jesus' clothes as he hung on the cross—as another example of the rich Jesus. Centurions would not have competed for a poor man's garments, he contends, but would more logically be expected to gamble for designer labels. (Pontius Hilfiger? Ralphius Lauren?)

Obviously, Dr. Norman knows his scripture. He's probably a big fan of Matthew, the lawyer/disciple who wrote "blessed are the poor in spirit," that great caveat that we Americans cling to, usually at the mall, when thinking about how best to max out our third credit card. (As opposed to that sourpuss Luke, the doctor/disciple who stopped at "blessed are the poor." Liberal.)

My personal favorite is the verse where Jesus talks about the eye of the needle, and how hard it is for a rich man to get through it, especially if he is a camel. Or something like that. It turns out the eye of the needle was actually a small opening in the outer wall of Jerusalem, a door only large enough for individuals to pass through. Actually, it sounds like the perfect place for an ATM. I mean, if you have to leave your camel on the outside, you might need a little cash to pay someone to watch it while you shop. I'm just sayin'.

THIS WHOLE Prosperity Gospel thing has certainly opened my eyes, and I look forward to hearing more of Dr. Robertson's interpretations of scripture, like the verse where Jesus told the rich man to "sell all he has and give it to the poor." (Probably a misprint.) Or Jesus' story about the widow who only gave a little—no offense, but not even a tithe—while the rich Pharisee gave a lot. Jesus told his disciples that the widow actually gave more, although how he came up with that I'm not sure. (Jesus: Prince of Peace? Absolutely. Math whiz? Not so much.) ∎

Investing or the Future

The economy continues to be in need of discussion, particularly since your 401k is turning out to be just the financial toilet you were once warned not to flush your money down into. But you continue to invest with of each paycheck, because experts insist that "dollar cost averaging"—or "flushing regularly"—is the best strategy for the long term.

For those unfamiliar with the term, "investing" essentially means saving money to buy things in the future that cost a lot less right now. (Both gasoline and milk, for example, are rising almost daily in price, leading one to the obvious solution of stockpiling them in the basement for a couple years—but not too close to the furnace, because the gas could go bad.)

Prudent financial planning has become a necessity since your parents are, at this very moment, blowing your well-unearned inheritance on frivolous things like food, medicine, and payments to Nigerian citizens who, because of their proud tradition of generosity, promise to return the money with interest just as soon as they figure out your parents' bank account number.

With the economy in apparent free-fall, investing wisely can be a challenging proposition. Fortunately, the age-old maxim of starting early still applies, as the following data show:

- If you are in the 25-to-35 age bracket, and set aside 5 percent of pre-tax income in stocks and bonds, your investments will grow—even if current economic conditions prevail—permitting you to retire comfortably by the age of 87.

- If you are in the 36-to-50 age group, you're behind already. You should immediately move into your neighbor's garage to save on rent and invest half of your salary in stocks of strong growth industries, such as prison construction. This will permit you to retire at 94, although you will still be required to work weekends. As a prison guard, perhaps.

- If, like me, you're in your late 50s, you should seriously consider selling your organs for cash. But remember— and this is important: You can sell a kidney, since you have two, but not a liver, which you only have one of. (Or maybe it's the other way around.)

AND AS YOU PLAN for the future, it is important to adhere to these three time-honored principles:

1) Always enter the Publishers Clearing House sweepstakes.

2) Don't travel without your lucky rabbit's foot.

3) Make regular contributions to a balanced portfolio of equity investments.

But why, one might ask, would you bother with that third thing, given the enormous potential of the first two? I mean, after decades of playing, what are the mathematical odds that you'll keep not winning the lottery?

I can only say that sticking to this forward-thinking philosophy has made me somewhat of a legend at my office. Staff members frequently stop by to seek out my financial counsel. As they listen carefully and take meticulous notes, they are humbled to be in the presence of a man who has been profoundly wrong in every financial decision he has ever made. They leave breathlessly determined to do the exact opposite of my advice, and to do it quickly, lest the forgetful mistakenly follow even my slightest suggestion. Such is the consistency of my investment record that my own father insists I call him before buying a stock, so he can dump it from his portfolio.

The tech stock crash of 2001? My fault. I bought Cisco Systems and then bragged about it, thus triggering a market correction that wiped out billions in assets.

The falling dollar? I blame myself. I called Europe and told them I was coming to visit.

Declining purchasing power? My bad. I recently told the hot dog vendor outside the Treasury Department downtown that his price for a half-smoke and chips seemed a little high. Next day's headline: "Fed Raises Rates on Rumors of Inflation!"

Fortunately, the Bible tells us we needn't worry about the future. Consider the lilies, it says, who neither toil nor spin (probably because they don't want to pull a hamstring). Not to mention the birds of the air, who "neither sow nor reap nor gather into barns," although, since they lack opposable thumbs, I wouldn't expect them to. Actually, it's been my observation that birds are incapable of anything except eating the seed I put out every morning. But as I sit at the breakfast table and watch them flitting about—and totally not sharing—I wonder if I'm just perpetuating their dependency or, worse, their sense of entitlement. It would be better if I taught them a skill, or perhaps a craft, such as constructing Russian nesting dolls out of macaroni noodles and paste, a practice that, given my financial acumen, may become a necessity in my own future. (Although I'm told that they make excellent gifts.) ▪

I am [pause for effect] ENVIRO-MAN!

(Editor's note: The following reveals "spoiler" information from the blockbuster movie Iron Man, another tediously derivative action film that's indistinguishable from other recent action films, except for the fact that it is just SO COOL!)

At a surprising moment in Iron Man, the principal character breaks the unwritten rule of superheroes and reveals his secret identity. For much of the movie he had fought evil concealed flying at supersonic speeds in a form-fitting metal suit which, if nothing else, was an advertisement for the need for talcum powder when wearing metal underwear.

Then, at the end of the film, he stands before the gathered media and just blurts out, "I'm Iron Man." The actor is Robert Downey Jr., who in real life has considerable experience standing before various groups, usually consisting of police or judges, and blurting out, with conviction, "Those aren't MY drugs," or "I promise to do better, if paroled."

The producers could have milked the secret identity thing for several sequels (after three episodes of Spider-Man, Peter Parker's secret identity is known only by his girlfriend and roughly 2 billion of the rest of us). Instead, they chose to reveal Iron Man's secret, apparently so he could share the loneliness of working for the common good without recognition or reward.

I understand this need. Because I, too, have a secret identity and have traveled across our great land working tirelessly not only for humankind, but for the very future of the planet itself. And now the truth can be told.

I am Enviro Man.

Or, possibly, Environment Man, or maybe EnvironMent-O, although that sounds like a breath mint, so forget that. When it comes to choosing your superhero name you've got to come up with one before the public takes a look at you, misses the point entirely, and assigns one of its own: "So, you're like, Leotard Boy, or what?"

Regardless, for the past 10 years my duty has been clear: I am an SUV's worst nightmare. To those gas-guzzling behemoths that destroy the ozone while masquerading as the family station wagon ... I am death.

Okay, so maybe not death, but I'm trying for some drama here. Mainly because there are those who think that my secret power—the ability to place accusatory stickers on the bumpers of offending vehicles—is not really much of a weapon, and certainly not a super-power. These skeptics insist I am not in the same league as, say, Superman or Wonder Woman, even though I once went to a Halloween party dressed as Wonder Woman and, to my credit, a few people actually didn't laugh so hard their soft drinks came out through their noses. In fact, to this small but insightful minority, I brought a certain dignity to the costume.

And it is that same dignity that I bring to my superhero duties, as I sneak—with dignity—around parking lots, crouch low behind bumpers, and stealthily flit from Chevy Suburban to Mercury Navigator to Hummer H3—vehicles that are some of the biggest contributors to global warning—leaving behind my brilliantly composed message of protest—"Big Car. Small Brain. This vehicle destroys the ozone, pollutes the air, and prolongs our dependence on foreign oil."

It's my way of saying, powerfully and unashamedly, "J'accuse!" Or, if grabbed from behind by the burly arms of an SUV owner—or her husband—I would add, with conviction, "Those aren't MY stickers!"

To my critics who claim you can't solve the world's problems by merely putting a sticker on them, I can only reply that, through no fault of my own, I have not been bitten by a radioactive spider, which scientists say gives you the strength of a spider, without the annoying side effects of those four extra legs. (If you had those, you'd need to drive around in an large vehicle, such as an SUV.) Nor, to continue my rebuttal, was I born on a distant planet with a red sun and a white-haired Marlon Brando as my dad.

So, frankly, stickering is the best I can do.

I STRIKE QUICKLY, in daylight or under cover of darkness, wearing the everyday clothing of an average American, which allows me to walk among the masses, undetected. I work alone, without the annoying and constant presence of a sidekick, although, if the need ever arose, I like the name "Enviro-Boy."

From New Mexico to Florida to upstate New York, I have bravely tagged offending vehicles with the Truth That Sticks, hoping the owners will drive unaware for several days, incriminating themselves to people in cars following close enough to read the inspiring words of Enviro Man: "Virginia Is For Lovers."

(No, not THAT bumper sticker! The other one!)

If you've ever found my sticker on your car, then shame on you for needing to be publicly mocked for driving such a wasteful car. (Although if you were the driver of that ambulance in Albuquerque, sorry about that. I put the sticker on your bumper before I looked up and realized the flashing lights might exempt the vehicle. Then I heard the muffled shouts of the paramedics trying to open the door from the inside but they couldn't, because I was in the way, you know, putting a sticker on the bumper.) ■

The Bible's Better Half
(*The Da Vinci Code* revisited)

The immensely popular book, *The Da Vinci Code* is a groundbreaking work that causes the reader to ask profoundly personal questions: Who did I loan my copy to and when will the five people they loaned it to give it back?

And that's not all. The book also challenges our basic understanding of biblical history and the theology that created the modern church. Even though The Da Vinci Code is a work of fiction (much like the upcoming biography *The Greatness of George W. Bush*), its descriptions of early church history are purportedly true, leaving the reader with the disturbing notion that the creation of the Bible itself was compromised by one major problem: They left out the good stuff.

According to The Da Vinci Code (and LOTS of respected academic literature, which I would have read but for my long-standing principle of being 100-percent research-free), the Roman emperor Constantine conspired with the early church hierarchy—which may have included Karl Rove—to create a set of scriptures that emphasized Jesus' divinity rather than his more accessible humanity. Whole parts of Jesus' life and legacy have been left out, depriving us of a fuller sense of what it must have been like to be the Son of God during, say, snack time in kindergarten. (TEACHER: Goodness me, where'd all those extra Cheerios come from?)

Nor do we have a record of his teenage years, a typically difficult time that youngsters today could better deal with had the biblical narrative included inspirational stories of an adolescent Jesus of Nazareth:

EDDIE OF HASKEL: Good morning, Mrs. Nazareth, is Jesus at home? And may I say you look lovely today. Having children at an early age certainly seems to have agreed with you.

JESUS: Cut it out, Eddie. And that reminds me, you are SO not going to be one of my disciples when I grow up.

EDDIE: Fine with me, Mr. Alpha and Omega Junior. Me and Lumpy have other plans anyway. We're going to be—get this— fishers of fish. As opposed to that wacky idea of yours.

JESUS: Whatever. Hey, Dad, can we take the car?

JOSEPH: What is a "car," my son?

JESUS: Oops. Never mind.

And while the Bible dwells on the 40 days of temptation before Jesus starts his ministry, we read nothing about the arguments he must have had with his teachers who probably wanted him to go to grad school first.

BUT THE BIGGEST problem with the Bible, according to The Da Vinci Code, is that it only tells half the story of the early church—the guy half—and omits much of the legacy of women. It's obvious the early church fathers didn't run their ideas by the early church ladies, probably for fear of having Third Century crockery flung at them in disgust. (In fact, some scientists believe the broken bits of pottery found in archeological digs were not the result of millennial decay, but were caused by angry women trying to keep priests away from the office shredders.)

I don't think I'm giving away the ending (since it's obvious by Chapter Two) to say that a particularly controversial aspect of the book, if true, would add a second shortest verse to the Bible. Specifically, "Jesus dated."

Let's face it, Constantine and his scribes couldn't have included scripture recounting Jesus' first social engagement with a girl (JESUS: Open thine eyes, and sin no more. GIRL: Look, I'm not really blind, okay? It's just an expression...), much less have the Bible making reference to the more controversial possibility that Jesus may have been married. (And it would have been the perfect marriage, with household chores that magically—okay, *divinely*—took care of themselves! Sigh.)

No, the state-sanctioned church wanted to keep Jesus above the people, so they would have to rely on the church to be the go-between for their salvation. Had the full story been told of Jesus' empowerment of his followers, today's ecclesial hierarchy would be mere comic relief, especially during high feast days. ("Nice hat [giggle] Your Holiness.")

As it is, the deeper experience of community and gender inclusiveness within the early church is little mentioned by scripture, and few other documents have survived to fill in these sinful omissions. All we have is the official Bible, the still unreleased Dead Sea Scrolls (TRANSLATOR: What's another word for "equal"? Oh, I know: "guys know best."), and some bits of parchment containing the earliest known recipe for Jell-O with miniature marshmallows. (Some Christian sects may have added coconut to this ancient potluck dish, but again, the flawed biblical record is unable to debunk this egregious heresy.)

Coconut...aaackk! ∎

An Epic Experience

I n the interest of cultural improvement, I have attempted
to better myself by reading *Remembrance of Things Past,*
considered by many literary critics to be the most brilliant
novel of the 20th century written by a guy named Marcel.

Proust's master work is 3,000 pages long, and I'm pleased
to report that, after only six weeks of daily reading, I'm already
up to page 32. (Yes, I've hit a slow patch, but I expect the author will pick up the pace in the last 2,968 pages.)

It's taking me a while because The Narrator—a wealthy
French boy waiting anxiously for his wealthy mother to come
up and kiss him good night—is describing, in exhaustive detail, the objects in his bedroom. This technique is used so that
the reader, presumably in preparation for major surgery, can
fall into a deep French expressionist coma. Either that, or it
was the writer's way of introducing us into the young man's
world which, given what he's describing, would take a really
long time to vacuum.

Not to second-guess one of the last century's greatest nov-
elists, but I wonder if the story might move along a bit faster
had the boy's bedroom suddenly lit up with the piercing flood-
lights of a hovering helicopter, and ninja-garbed figures rappelled down and crashed through the windows. This would
have the valuable literary effect of scaring the crap out of the
kid and taking his mind off his momma. It would also propel
the reader into the next chapter, which hopefully would in-

clude political intrigue, betrayal, and a car chase.

But I am no stranger to books of substance and consequence. My bookshelves at home are filled with them. *Theological Ethics,* Helmut Thielicke's brilliant three-volume series on the implied dialectic of freedom and bondage, occupies by far the largest amount of space on my bookshelf. Which is why I moved it the other day when I dropped my slinky. I occasionally use this device to entertain the pets—since my family has developed a keen lack of appreciation for my skills—and I was shocked to distraction by the sight of our rabbit attempting to "be romantic" with one of the cats. That's when I lost control of the slinky and it dropped onto the bookshelf behind several other books that I have never read but which also look good in italics, including *New Testament Greek for Dummies, John Calvin: The Years of Laughter,* and *A Bunch of My Wife's College Textbooks.*

READING PROUST is just one of the ways I've been trying to improve my cultural life. Recently I agreed to attend a poetry reading, primarily because I was unable to come up with a reason not to. I have traditionally avoided these events since they lack the competitive quality of other culturally uplifting activities—such as professional wrestling—and rarely include the chips and beer that should be required at poetry readings of any real distinction.

By happy coincidence, this particular gathering included what was probably the best buffet I have ever made a complete fool of myself enjoying. We're talking strawberries the size of tennis balls, Brie to die for, and cinnamon pita points that were so crisp and tasty I had to be restrained from going back for seconds. (Although, to be perfectly honest, I was already on thirdsies.) Unfortunately the plates were the size of coasters, which required an acute sense of balance. Hint: pita point, Brie slice, then strawberry. Repeat. Fortunately, I had my shirt pocket for back-up.

To make matters worse, the food was laid out directly behind the podium, which meant that saying "oh yummy" after each new discovery became a major distraction to the poets. Although during one reading, my spontaneous lip-smacking actually provided a touch of the iambic that, to this listener, was sorely needed.

From my vantage point at the buffet table—between bites of crunchy pita—I was able to pay close attention to the readings, and I determined that, despite a wide range of topics, the amateur poets seemed to draw from the same inspirational categories, namely:

- Clouds.
- A deeply moving personal tragedy.
- More clouds.

(I'm told that amateur poets like clouds because they look like cotton candy in the sky.)

Despite people shushing me and tugging my sleeves at the buffet table, I came away from the experience inspired to revisit my own poetic efforts for literary magazines. Unfortunately, two of my early works—"Hooray for Water" and "Unicycles Make Me Smile"—had been cruelly rejected by editors whose master's degrees and long experience in the field provides, in my opinion, the barest of qualifications to judge. I admit that my earlier works may have lacked a certain scope and depth, but my latest effort reveals a more mature poet at work. It is my opus, as fresh as today's headlines, as timeless as an epic novel, only shorter. I call it "What's the Deal With Cell Phones?"

What's the Deal With Cell Phones?

What's the deal with cell phones? Anyhow?
People talk on them
All the time. And then they make calls
While they're driving
Under the clouds.

Hard to improve such verse, unless, while you were reading it, helicopters swooped down from overhead and ninjas burst through your window. That would be cool. ■

News Flash:
El Nino Leads to Hair Loss

Whew. I was afraid it was hereditary, since, in social settings, my paternal grandfather gave the appearance of well-polished cue ball. (At home, he just looked like a regular cue ball.) But now that scientists have proven that baldness is weather-related, I only have to worry about it during hurricane season.

And speaking of El Niño, how out of touch are the weather doofuses (doofi?) who came up with *that* name? "A global weather phenomenon with the most destructive potential of anything on the planet? Hey, let's call it 'the little boy' in Spanish." You'd think there'd be a more appropriate name for something that causes tidal waves, hurricanes, and massive flooding. Such as "Green-Eyed Monster" or "Here Comes Death." Or maybe "Newt Gingrich."

Ironically, those same scientists have also discovered that El Niño causes temporary memory loss. Which accounts for my forgetting to buy a gift for our 20th wedding anniversary (although, at press time, she wasn't buying the El Niño excuse.)

I can be forgiven for thinking that a whole weekend together at an ocean-front bed and breakfast WOULD BE ENOUGH, THANK YOU! But apparently something in a decoratively wrapped box was also expected. Which is another reminder that after two decades living in the District of Columbia (oops, I mean state of marital bliss) I can still get it wrong.

Like the other day, when she asked me to let the cat in and did not know the cat had a mouse in his mouth. (He was standing at the door going "meowfth, meowfth.") I let him in anyway because she asked me to. That was a mistake. Or maybe just a difference in perspective, which is often the source of tension in a marriage. That's why a long time ago we took one of those personality profile tests which show couples that, in marriage, it's not a matter of right or wrong, but the simple fact that some people just see things differently. (I, for example, usually see the glass as half full. My wife, on the other hand, sees the glass as very dirty and why didn't I vacuum the living room yesterday when I was supposed to?)

The result of our profile tests revealed my wife to be a reflective, intuitive, and sensitive woman. My test revealed that I should have pressed down harder on the No. 2 pencil.

WE HAD HIGH HOPES for our anniversary weekend, which was spent eight miles off the mainland on a small island accessible only by boat. And not a big boat. A little tiny boat designed by sadistic craftsmen who wanted tourists to experience every wave, every dip and yaw and surge that little tiny boats feel on the open sea.

Of course, eight miles only takes about 10 minutes in a car with solid highway beneath you. But on the ocean (did I mention it was a little boat?) that same distance takes almost an hour. An hour of dipping, and yawing and surging, and dipping and yawing, and that was on a calm day. On the way back we sailed through a storm, which meant the YAWING and DIPPING and SURGING were in capital letters. It also meant that halfway across I got so scared that I violated several commandments by praying to any god within the sound of my voice just to get us through. As the waves tossed us onto the floor of the boat, my life started to pass before me: all the joys, all the fears, all the lies my parents told me about me being a little teapot. And in the midst of the storm I realized, finally, that I am not now, nor have I ever been, short or stout. I have no handle. I have no spout, despite my being forced to sing otherwise, and...."Okay folks, we're here," said the captain, ending my hallucinatory near-death experience with a solid bump into the dock.

Ironically that boat ride resulted in the most romantic part of the whole weekend: We both kissed the ground when we stepped onto the shore.

But the bed and breakfast was beautiful, a perfect place for a weekend of romance, and togetherness, and rain. It rained all weekend. But that was okay, because we brought a book by Thich Nhat Hanh, the Vietnamese author who writes about the mindfulness of the moment, about living in the present and seeing each second of life as a gift to be savored and appreciated. It was a great book and we couldn't wait to finish it.

The first night (before the rain started) provided a picture-perfect scene: my wife sitting comfortably under the folds of a warm blanket, reading a book on a porch that looked out over the bay. She might have been pondering the bliss of her marriage, or reflecting on that moment in her life when she thought a weak chin, thick glasses, and a stutter were attractive on a man. (Be honest, you once had a crush on Don Knots, didn't you?)

But mainly she was just trying to ignore her husband who was a few yards away, leaning over the edge of a wooden dock, attempting to return a crab cake lunch back to the sea from which it came. (Note to seafood restaurants: Mayonnaise should be refrigerated periodically to prevent customers having to spend the first night of their anniversary prostrate on a dock-—albeit a romantically moonlit dock-—making sounds that frighten the waterfowl.)

But as we move into the third century of our marriage (Oops. Hah, hah! I meant third decade...), we look forward to our twilight years together, enjoying long walks, and good books, and a time to talk about things, such as how to get our pampered and ungrateful daughters to move out of the house since they'll be almost 50. "But Dad, we like it here," they'll say as I hobble by on my cane. "By the way, have you finished our laundry yet?" ∎

Pompous and Circumstantial

This month I'll join with thousands of proud fathers across the country in celebrating our children's college graduation, a major milestone in a journey that will be marked by opportunities, challenges, and, hopefully, the ability to pay for their own food.

It will be an emotional event, one that my family has insisted must not be marred by me muttering "one down, one to go" as I sit in the audience. I'll have enough on my mind anyway, because my feet will be soaking wet from slushy sidewalks typical of your picturesque upstate New York college towns in late May. Contrary to weather systems in other regions, these towns have only three seasons:

- fall

- more fall

- pneumonia

The proud grandparents will be there, of course, as well as sundry relatives including my wife's in-laws, a rowdy bunch of Republicans with whom I'm often accused of turning every gathering into a political free-for-all. I deny this, just as the Bush administration denies its shameless gutting of environmental protections, a fact I'll be sure to point out just before the "pomp" or slightly after the "circumstance."

Our daughter has worked hard for this moment, tackling

her studies with an intensity that can only come from trying to get everything done before the spring formal. She wrote her papers, made the grades, and, with her new degree in French and International Relations, she'll soon be ready to tackle any challenge the food service industry can throw at her.

Okay, that was a little harsh. Actually, she's been offered a job in environmental advocacy, a position she accepted only because, she assured me, the jobs in the high-paying field of obscure humor writers were already taken. The good news is that, despite her modest salary, she'll actually be in a higher tax bracket than, say, General Electric, a company that paid no taxes in three of the last four years. (Sorry. Just practicing for the relatives.)

I HAD HOPED to personally deliver this year's commencement address, engaging the young graduates with inspirational examples from my own life that have, at a minimum, qualified me for prizes with names like Nobel, Pulitzer, and Publishers Clearinghouse. But the college declined my offer, choosing instead a person of "known academic accomplishment," which I took as a cheap shot at my associate of arts degree. (I was unjustly denied a bachelor's by the archaic requirement that students actually attend class their senior year.) I thought I might still have a shot when I learned that a famous name is another qualification for commencement speakers. In the end, however, it wasn't enough that my co-workers call me "Condoleeza."

THE ONE THING that could mar this joyful occasion is the moment when I present my daughter with the bill for her first 21 years. Right now, it comes to $314,742.92, although, being the loving and generous parent that I am, I'll call it an even three hundred thou.

I hadn't planned to ask for repayment, but money is a little tight now that the federal government has turned down my request to forgive her college loans. Apparently—and this may surprise some of you parents—federal loans must be repaid even if the graduate is smart and cute! I know, I know. This was a shock to me, too. (I even sent photos.) Apparently, a young person's promise to go into the world with energy, enthusiasm, and a new set of luggage is not enough to inspire generosity from an ungrateful government. I suggested she change her name to Lockheed Martin and then just send a bill, since the government doesn't think twice about paying those. But she decided against it after realizing she might eventually have to cooperate with congressional investigators. (She said she wants to focus on the "future, not the past," which is often what year hear on Capitol Hill when defense contractors accused of bilking the government wonder out loud why a simple "Look, we're sorry". Can't we just leave it at that?" doesn't seem to satisfy.)

Be that as it may, our troubled world needs its young people, and this year's graduates can be counted on to make it a better place. As long as they can do it on Facebook. While listening to an iPod.

And it all begins at graduation, when the graduating class turns toward its teary-eyed parents (some with wet feet) and presents itself to the world. That emotional moment will culminate with the traditional toss of the mortar boards, giving parents a final glimpse of unexpectedly bizarre behavior that, for the last four years, we've just assumed they've indulged in every weekend. But that moment will be lost on me, since I intend to push my way through the crowd and catch my daughter's cap before it hits the ground.

It's a rental. ■

Running on Empty

Keep 'em laughing, I always say, especially when you're half-naked on a gurney surrounded by stern-looking nurses. So when one of them asked if I had completely flushed out my system the night before and hadn't eaten that morning, I cleverly responded: "Nothing but that Burrito Breakfast Special down at the Taco Bell. Otherwise, I'd be REAL hungry right now! Hahahahha!"

(Editor's note: Please, not again. Not another tedious recounting of your latest medical procedure. For years we've had to suffer through every paper cut, every fearful encounter with a stinging insect, every heart "incident." Can you just give it a rest!?)

Nor did I leave the doctors out of the pre-colonoscopy fun, gently chiding them at their choice of medical specialty with comments such as, "So, you guys studied for years and years so you could, like, do this every day for the rest of your professional lives, right? Right?"

Doctors (whispering among themselves): "Get out the old hose. The one that's a little jaggedy on the end."

Like I always say, laughter is the best sedative!

(Editor's note: Look, as we speak there are hundreds of thousands of immigrants protesting for their rights in cities across this country, and all you want to talk about is your colon!?)

That's an excellent point about a very important issue.

Despite our nation's history of welcoming the outsider, many Americans now feel that our country is filling up with foreigners beyond our capacity to contain them all.

Much like the bloated feeling I got the night before my colonoscopy.

Admittedly, I did not think about the issues dividing our nation as I sat in the bathroom forcing down two gallons of ill-flavored laxative. The liquid was prescribed to purge my body of all substances, illegal or otherwise, but to be honest, for most of the evening the political metaphors were lost on me.

(Editor's Note: Oh SPARE US! There's a WAR on, for heaven's sake! And it's a quagmire. After four years there just doesn't seem to be a way out. Iraq is still not a country that can stand on its own.)

Nor could I, now that you mention it. Oh, I tried to cut and run, but I kept returning, ultimately trapped, unable to leave the bathroom for any reason. Although I wouldn't call it a "quagmire." (I'm not sure where the editors are going with that, unless they're referring to the president when he said, "We're not leaving until the job is finished." THAT I can relate to. I mean, you just can't set a timetable on this sort of thing.)

But you'll be happy to know that the day after the procedure the doctors reported that I was—in medical parlance—"as clean as a whistle." And to prove it they showed me pictures of my actual insides, which I couldn't wait to put up on our refrigerator when I got home. (However, despite my exemplary results and the excellent resolution of the full-color photos, some have suggested I not display the pictures on this page. They were concerned about something called "projectile vomiting" and the fact that some squeamish readers might not be ready to celebrate what a really healthy intestine looks like.)

Actually, a photo of the procedure is much better than what

I woke up to in the recovery room following my childhood tonsillectomy. I was 3 years old, and I groggily turned my head to see, on the bedside table next to me, a clear jar containing my actual tonsils floating in some kind of liquid. They looked like space alien embryos. Trying to get out. Apparently, hospitals sending patients home with their surgically-removed organs was what they did back in 1953. Fortunately, this practice is now banned under the Geneva Convention.

BEFORE I LEFT the doctor's office, they insisted that I also look at pictures of a bad colon, presumably as a deterrent for cancer-causing behavior, such as opening up the Arctic National Wildlife Preserve to oil production. (Okay, not really.) Medical professionals do not think highly of people who live the high-risk lifestyle associated with consuming fatty foods, alcohol, and other things that are delicious and fun. Because when you live like that, what you get is polyps. And polyps can cause cancer, which was bad enough to think about. But then the doctors insisted on showing me how these gross little bumps attach themselves to your intestinal wall and, depending on the angle of the light, look like either failed al Qaeda member Zacarias Moussaoui or former Minnesota Gov. Jesse "The Polyp" Ventura. (Think about these guys the next time you're considering a Whopper.)

BY THE WAY, a friend of mine pointed out that Bill Clinton may have had sex with an intern in the White House, but George W. Bush is giving a colonoscopy to the entire country.
    Or words to that effect. ■

An Innocent in
the Land of Facebook

I t started innocently enough. An acquaintance e-mailed me and, using a new verb with which I was unfamiliar, asked if she could "friend" me. Considering she was already a friend, her request was not readily understood. Is the verb "friend" more intimate than the noun version? Will this involve touching? Should I consult a priest or parole officer before replying?

Being the trusting individual that I am, I clicked on the link in her e-mail, followed the on-screen instructions to fill out a few lines of personal information—name, gender, criminal record—and clicked again. My life hasn't been the same since. It was as if I had walked through the back of a wardrobe and emerged in a snow-covered woods illuminated by a single lamppost, against which leaned a huge and menacing ape-like monster with only one eye. (Sorry. Sometimes I get that Narnia book mixed up with *Lord of the Rings*.)

Apparently, I had signed up for something called "Facebook," a virtual universe where people stay in touch with each other on a daily basis with—and this must be some kind of Facebook rule—the most banal humdrum that simply *must* be shared. "I'm having coffee and reading the paper," a friend writes on her page, an idle comment that God Almighty—who knows all and sees all—would probably fail to note, but which nonetheless triggers an automatic e-mail telling all her friends that she has just "updated" her page. This is now archived into a permanent space on the World Wide Web, despite the fact it would be of interest only to a parent ("What, you can read the paper but you can't call your *mother*?") or criminal investigators looking for behavioral clues as to why, after finishing the newspaper, she walked out of her house carrying a meat cleaver.

Far worse, an incoming Facebook alert triggers one's inner zombie. You can't *not* click on the link, enter your password, and wait expectantly, because a friend could be informing you she has an incurable disease, or has been appointed to the Obama administration, or just received a MacArthur genius grant. Nope. Just drinking coffee.

Who invented this? It's pen pals from hell, but without the collectible foreign postage stamps.

After "friending" the first person, I got another request. A month later I'm up to 97 Internet friends, some with names I recognize, others that are familiar but whose faces are not. Being new to this universe, I simply "confirmed" any new friend that came along, praying that I would not, at some future date, have to write stuff in all their yearbooks.

But can I trust these new "friends"? Are there junk friends on Facebook like the junk e-mail I regularly get? Do advertisers pose as friends, so when I "friend" them I inadvertently sign up for vinyl siding, or a new cell phone, or a speed-dating seminar?

And what if someone asks me to friend them but I don't want to? A colleague says just ignore their request but never, under any circumstances, click the "Ignore" button, because that could offend them. And they might come after you with a cleaver.

And dare I invite someone to be *my* friend? What if they

don't want me as their Facebook buddy? What if they click "Ignore" and suddenly it's high school all over again? Do I need this in the autumn (okay, early winter) of my life?

See how much anxiety this is creating for me? (Should I get a date for prom now, or wait until later?) Suddenly, I'm an insecure teenager again, but without the comforting cowboy-themed bedroom in which to take refuge.

THE ARCHITECTURE OF Facebook—not to mention the vernacular—is also confusing. Apparently I have a "wall" that people can write things on ("I'm going shopping, then to a Save Darfur rally, then back to shopping"), but I don't see anything that looks like a wall on my page. Just lots of photos and quotations from people ("Okay, I'm back. Good rally. Now off to Target!"). And if people put something on my "wall," can I take it off without turpentine? Frankly, I'd rather they just spray-paint something on the side of my neighbor's garage. A lot easier to read, and then I could clean it off.

And since being on Facebook basically means having your own Internet site, it takes hours each day to maintain, most of which must be done during the work day to avoid using personal time at home. This may not go over with the boss, so make sure you keep a computer game in the background of your monitor at all times. That way, if someone walks by, you can quickly change your screen to the game, so people know you're actually working. ■

A Selfless Act of Love

I pulled dramatically into the office parking lot, turned off the ignition and coasted to a stop, the powerful engine reluctantly emitting its final throaty rumble. A co-worker walked over and asked, "Mid-life crisis?"

"Not any more," I replied, pulling off the black full-face racing helmet and tossing my hair from side to side in cinematic slow-motion, forgetting, for the moment, that I have no hair to toss—only glasses, which went flying off my face and ended up under the dumpster.

Okay, so the drama of the moment was lost. Plus, without my glasses I had to ask my co-worker to help my foot locate the kickstand. For lesser men, such events might have muted the power of their entrance, but I was undeterred. As I stepped off the bike, my black leather jacket creaking seductively, I knew it was time to strut into the office with the swagger and pride reserved for that most unique of American icons: The Motorcycle Man.

But first I had to find my glasses.

Despite accusing me of having somebody else's shoulders, my colleagues were generally impressed at my new persona. As I walked by (dramatically), with helmet in hand, I was pleased to hear their snickering whispers of deep respect.

Now, before you jump to the wrong conclusion, it must be said that getting a motorcycle was not the selfish act of a middle-aged man struggling with a sense of his own inadequacies. No, it was purely an expression of love for a family which, I feared, had become woefully out of balance. Consider the facts: My wife teaches autistic children, our youngest daughter works with orphans in Honduras, and our oldest is a passionate organizer and fund-raiser for the environment. In the face of such rampant selflessness, a corrective was clearly needed. The scales cried out to be balanced. Happily, I can report that my family is pleased and, dare I say, grateful, that I intervened.

When I first announced my plans at the dinner table, the daughters were unanimous. "Cool," they declared, turning immediately to the mother, who was somewhat less verbal in her response. With the fork paused in midair and her eyes widened, it was clear she could barely contain her enthusiasm. As she began to slowly shake her head, I could see that she was mourning the fact that our 25 years of marriage had never included a motorcycle.

And who can blame her? After all, motorcycles are fun to ride and provide a great transportation alternative to cars and their annoyingly comfortable seats. Plus, they have several advantages over automobiles, such as eliminating the need for time-consuming windshield maintenance.

Motorcycle riders sit up higher than most vehicles, so they are more visible to drivers of oncoming cars, unless those drivers are talking on their cell phones, which they always are, so forget that one.

When you hit a pothole in a car and get a flat tire, it can take as long as an hour to change it. But when a motorcycle hits a pothole, particularly at highway speeds, the paramedics do all the work, as you wait patiently in a relaxing coma, or peer down euphorically from the branches of a nearby tree.

Not to mention the superior fuel efficiency of a motorcycle, or the convenience of having the gas tank and its three gallons of highly flammable liquid placed right there between your legs.

And a motorcycle builds community, particularly when it falls over during a parking mishap. At 500 pounds, it takes a small group of passersby to help pick it up. Likewise, while car drivers are struggling with steering wheel locks, a motorcycle can easily be secured with a simple 100-pound logging chain, as long as those same passers-by are still around to help lift it.

Of course, adjusting to a different driving style can take a little time, especially when your first instinct is to stop by dragging your feet, Fred Flintstone-like, at 30 miles per hour. (Just for the record, this doesn't work.) And becoming part of the motorcycle mystique takes some getting used to. Being the envy of every man—and the secret desire of every woman—is an enormous responsibility, and one must not take advantage of the social prestige that comes so naturally to a man riding a quarter ton of steel. For decades, our society has held a special place for such men and has, on occasion, put them there.

But enough about the penitentiary. The hardest adjustment for me was learning the unwritten code of the road which, among other things, requires that motorcyclists acknowledge each other by unspoken means. When approaching another man on a bike (we call them "bikes," they're not bikes, but we call them that), the code requires a subtle lifting of the left hand followed by a casual pointing toward the road. No eye contact is made, and the eyes stare straight ahead behind opaque and unbelievably cool sunglasses. Unaware of this practice my first day out, however, I waved at other motorcyclists like a Santa in the Christmas parade. I even waved at a guy on a scooter, an unforgiveable act of folly. Fortunately a nice fellow Harley rider pulled me aside and kindly pointed out my error. Then he slapped me around a little bit. (Apparently, the reason those black leather jackets are so large is so they can accommodate the swelling that often comes from such kindly instruction.)

THE IMPORTANT THING is that only on a motorcycle can you experience the thrill of the open road and the limitless horizon that stretches out ahead. It's just you, the highway, and the shopping list for the grocery store three blocks away.

But make no mistake, a man's life cannot be fulfilled by material possessions, nor is his value to loved ones enhanced by machines of sport or pleasure. Of course not. When a man reaches midlife and begins to question his worth or doubt his accomplishments, it takes much more than a motorcycle to reaffirm his sense of self.

For that you need a jet ski. ∎

A Different Word for Everything!

International travel provides valuable cross-cultural experiences that give us a glimpse of the incredible beauty of our world and its peoples. Not that I need this personally, mind you, since I'd rather stay home in my pajamas and watch *Seinfeld* reruns. But this changed when I recently accompanied family members to Honduras, a country that is nowhere near my house.

Our youngest daughter has been busy qualifying for sainthood the past few years by working at an orphanage for children with HIV outside San Pedro Sula (Spanish for "hot, like Hell, only more humid") and has long wanted her parents to join her for a week's visit. Not much of a traveler myself, I was persuaded to make the trip only after being lured out to the front porch to see a pretty butterfly, at which point I was handcuffed and thrown into the trunk of our car. (Okay, I made up the part about the handcuffs. But I still have spare tire marks on my pajamas.)

Anyway, Honduras is a lovely country, if you can get past the fact that few, if any, of its residents can speak intelligibly. At least to me. English is my first language, my native tongue, and by coincidence, also my back-up language. Both have served me well in the times when multilingualism is important, such as when ordering a cheeseburger in Washington, D.C. But things are different in Honduras, a nation whose citizens stubbornly refused to comprehend me, even when I talked louder.

My own feeble attempts at actually speaking Spanish were complicated by the idiomatic peculiarities of the language. For example, "I love you" and "I'll call you" are phonetically similar, so much so that when I innocently asked the hotel clerk about using the telephone, I noticed that he blushed, winked, and sighed deeply with anticipation. And when, after a particularly enjoyable restaurant meal I complimented the cook on having the "best kitchen in Honduras" I was told I had actually told her she was a large pig. (This was the same restaurant with the balcony that looked over the nearby picturesque rooftops, the nearest one of which was where a cat had chosen to eat a mouse, a dead mouse, that he had apparently been saving for a special occasion. This coincided with the exact moment they brought our meal which, unlike the mouse, went mostly uneaten.)

Being misunderstood in English is probably better than saying the wrong thing in Spanish. So I reverted to simply listening appreciatively to a language that has the rhythmically fluid sound of sweet syrup being poured on a warm afternoon. By comparison, American English sounds like coughing up a hairball, impolitely. It's no longer a mystery to me that the Latin-based tongues are called "romance" languages, best employed to describe the hue of a woman's eyes or the beauty of an equatorial sunset, while English is what you use to talk to the cable guy.

Fortunately, my daughter is a fluent Spanish speaker and better able to participate in what appears to be the delightful Honduran sense of humor, given that most of the conversations ended with everyone in the room turning toward me and laughing, presumably in a sign of deep cross-cultural respect.

HONDURAS is a nation rich in Mayan history, which apparently includes Cinnabon, the pastry franchise found on almost every city block. This may explain why ancient temple doorways, though short, were extra wide.

In the daily commute from our hotel we traveled mainly by taxi, which contained neither seatbelts nor, in some cases, floors. But to their credit, the drivers minimized our exposure to danger by driving REALLY FAST. This also improved my prayer life considerably.

Most of our time was spent at the Casa Corazón, the orphanage where I expected to find a ward of weakened toddlers in their sick beds. This notion dissolved quickly when, upon arrival, I was set upon by two dozen giggling children who seemed to have made a wager beforehand about how many of themselves they could stack on Señor New Guy. (Answer: The knees started to buckle at about 12.) The children are small, because the HIV has slowed their growth, but other than twice-daily medications (the toddlers sat in a line against the wall—so cute!), they are typical children. Meaning, they derived the same perverse satisfaction from seeing grown-ups squirm. Turns out, these kids weren't hungry for attention, they wanted entertainment, and fortunately I was prepared to comply on the highest order. In all modesty, never has the detachable thumb trick been so well received, nor the vanishing coin—which reappears magically in the ear of a nearby child—so loudly applauded. American audiences might have scoffed at the tightly honed marvels of "Edwardo el Magnifico," but not these children, who knew real talent when it babbled at them unintelligibly.

SPEAKING SERIOUSLY, I had never seen desperate poverty before I visited Casa Corazón's village—nor have I seen so much hope. Nor, for that matter, have I seen so many chickens tied to the back of bicycles. But that's beside the point, which is as follows: Spending a week with laughing and loving children who may never reach adulthood didn't evoke the pity I expected to feel. Instead it filled me with an intense appreciation for the now, and a stubborn hope for tomorrow. I was in awe of these children who giggle and hug and live with voraciousness, and of the staff who work tirelessly in 100-degree heat. I fell in love with all of them.

(But don't tell a certain hotel clerk. It would break his heart.) ∎

Seriously,
Is This What Hell Is Like?

After less than a year of violin lessons, I am already reaping the rewards of music training. Before my instruction, I didn't know the difference between Brahms and Beethoven. Now, as a classically trained musician, I know that Beethoven has more letters than Brahms, not to mention two more syllables.

Despite this newfound knowledge and confidence, I was ill-prepared to hear it was time for my first public recital. This ludicrous suggestion, monstrous in its presumptiveness, was made by a fiend whom we shall call, simply, The Violin Teacher.

Recovering speech, I asked if "Mary Had a Little Lamb," played very slowly, would be acceptable for my debut. The fiend turned, a sadistic twinkle in his eye—if, in fact, fiends can twinkle—and placed two pages on the music stand. It was "Concerto No. 5," by Friedrich Seitz, a German composer who suffered from a unique form of dementia, the symptoms of which include putting excessive numbers of notes on a page and, having done so, putting them REAL close together.

(And what's the deal with using numbers instead of names for classical pieces? Was Beethoven so exhausted after composing his masterpiece that all he had left was "Okay, the last one was 'Symphony No. 4,' so I'll call this one, um, 'No. 5'"?

Why not something evocative, like "Winter's Morn is a Breakin' Over a Mist-Shrouded Lake," or "My Achy Breaky Hearth"? Or, in the case of Seitz's "Concerto No. 5," "Tchyeah, Like You Could Play This.")

I had six weeks to prepare, six short weeks to come up with the precise medical condition that would, sadly, force me to stay home the day of the recital. "It's probably the bug that's been going around," I would speak into my teacher's voicemail, unless he picked up the phone, in which case I would breathe heavily, mumble something about cholera, and hang up.

Short of this, however, my only consolation was that I was not required to invite anyone to the recital, which, if people asked, would be held at an undisclosed location. (Actually, it was in a church, an apparently godless place where my desperate prayers for deliverance went unheeded. In fact, I think I saw God sitting in the back row, giggling when it was my turn to perform.)

IN FAIRNESS TO my teacher, he tried to prepare me as best he could. He stressed that, when playing before an audience, it is absolutely crucial to try really, REALLY HARD ... to relax. To the non-musician, this may seem counterintuitive. But to me, an experienced student of the violin, it is completely idiotic. "Trying hard" and "relaxing" are two different universes. It's not apples and oranges. It's apples and small appliances. Relaxing comes from being comfortable and has nothing to do with perspiring profusely, which was the second thing I did when I arrived for the recital. The first thing was attempt to run over my violin while parking the car, but I got the angle wrong. So I blew that excuse.

I WAS PLACED AT the end of the program, presumably to allow more time for the blood to rush to my head, my palms to sweat, and a nervous twitch to develop in my left eye. Add to these my recent discovery that, while playing intently, I sometimes drool out of the right side of my mouth, and I knew I would make a strong impression on the 100 or so people at hand.

When my name was finally called, I stood and slowly approached the podium, and I'm pretty sure I heard someone whisper "dead man walking" as I passed by. I faced the audience, a sea of nameless faces, mainly parents of the younger performers who—and I don't want to brag here—were much shorter than me. I brought the instrument to my shoulder and waited for the pianist to finish his lengthy and exuberant introduction, the kind of introduction that suggested that something really special was about to happen. By the way, this was easy for him because, unlike me, he had been practicing since the 20th century.

My teacher nodded for me to begin, and that's the last thing I remember. I vaguely recall making a sort of flailing movement with my bow (note to musicians: This technique is patent-pending, so I'll expect royalties if you use it), then feeling a massive change in barometric pressure that filled my ears with the sound of rushing water. A polite applause broke through when I had apparently finished, either shortly before or long after the pianist stopped. And then my feet walked me back to my seat.

A glance at my instructor's eyes revealed that I had been either stupifyingly bad or just this side of awful. The pianist just stared wide-eyed, his mouth open, although—and I'm just guessing here—I don't think he was about to cry out "Genius!"

I quietly put my instrument away, relieved that the ordeal was over and confident that, even though this wasn't a competition and the performers tried their very best, I definitely had the best violin case. ∎

APPENDICES

(That's plural for "appendix," which, if you begin to experience extreme abdominal pain, you should probably have removed by a licensed physician. Although we hear that Home Depot has this new tool...)

Like most introductions to books, appendix pages are similarly disregarded. "Hey, if it was important, the author would have squeezed it in earlier," say the voices of bored college students, as they briefly look up from their video games. And these pages are no different. In fact, the author suggests if you *must* read them, at least watch a video game while doing it. The reason is that the following pages contain material which is either too painful to read (such as unnecessarily revisiting the political origins of George W. Bush or, worse, Dan Quayle), too personal to appreciate, or too religious to comprehend, unless you understand our need to occasionally placate an angry God.

Dan Quayle: Rested and Ready

(Editor's Note: I know, I know: Why pick on him now, after all these years? Why not just let sleeping dogs lie or, in the case of Dan Quayle, let over-paid private equity fund managers rot in jail. But that doesn't quite have the same ring, does it? By the way, can you believe that after being a political laughing stock Quayle was hired by a major Wall Street investment firm? Seriously, would you bet your retirement on a man who has the intellect of an American flag lapel pin? Come to think of it, has anybody asked where Dan Quayle was during the collapse of Wall Street? Was he anywhere near a computer?

(But history, as has been found elsewhere in this book, has much to teach us, especially if read aloud in bars, which, we're told, many readers did with this column.)

"What a waste it is to lose one's mind. Or, not to have a mind is being very wasteful. How true that is." Tough words from a tough man. The man: Dan Quayle. The words: I have no idea. But they were spoken with the seriousness and confidence

that can only come from a selfless public servant who once said, "I stand by all the misstatements that I've made."

Forgetting for the moment that being president is a speaking part, Dan Quayle, the heir-transparent to George Bush's teeny little legacy, has announced his candidacy for the highest office in the land. Or, to use his own words, "It's not the highest in altitude, of course, since a mountain is much higher than that. And you wouldn't put an office on a mountain, because all your memo thingies would blow away." Okay, I just made that up (or I could put it on the Internet and then it would be true). But I didn't make up this one: "I have made good judgments in the past. I have made good judgments in the future."

Yes, Dan Quayle is back, and I know I speak for pundits everywhere when I say how much I've missed him. People can criticize the media for being secular, but I'm telling you the idea of having Dan Quayle back on the campaign trail is causing journalists to fall on their knees in religious fervor, thanking God for the bounty of His or Her blessings. Writers who previously only used the name of Jesus Christ with the middle initial "H" are now giving all credit to the risen Lord who, in his mercy and divine sense of humor, has rolled away the stone of political reason and brought Dan Quayle back from the dead.

Instead of sleeping through the rhetorical sparrings of Steve *Forbes* (or is it Steve *Business Week*?) and whichever of the Bush brothers is running (is it Jeb, or his other brother Jeb?), now we have the prospect of Dan Quayle being up there on the dais. And SAYING STUFF! Like this: "Republicans understand the importance of bondage between a mother and child."

Ooooh! What looked to be an extremely dull presidential campaign now has the potential to make newspaper readers spontaneously spew breakfast coffee over their entire families as they check out what the master soliloquist said the night before.

As a reminder of what lies ahead, let's review the record of a man who has already stated clearly his positions on the bread and butter issues of the day. And, who, if asked, would not hesitate to demonstrate by spreading butter all over his hand and then getting a piece of bread out and forcefully declaring, "No, that's not right—I think you get the bread out first and then spread on the butter."

But seriously, Dan Quayle has spoken—and spoken clearly—as this brief summary of his actual words reveals:

"The future will be better tomorrow. But we don't want to go back to tomorrow. We want to go forward."

"We're going to have the best-educated American people in the world."

"I believe we are on an irreversible trend toward more freedom and democracy—but that could change."

"One word sums up the responsibility of any vice president, and that one word is 'to be prepared.'"

"It isn't pollution that's harming the environment. It's the impurities in our air and water that are doing it."

"I love California. I practically grew up in Phoenix."

"I was recently on a tour of Latin America, and the only regret I have was that I didn't study Latin harder in school so I could converse with those people."

(Stop. STOP! I'm spewing coffee over my entire family!)

"Words are THE MOST important part of language. Without words you couldn't talk and you can't have language without talking. Not to mention words." That's the kind of rhetoric we can expect during the Quayle candidacy, even though he didn't say that. But that's the kind of rhetoric I'm prepared to make up if he lets us down and suddenly becomes cogent or glib. We can't have that. Which is why our shameless mockery of Dan Quayle has to be only slightly shameless with just a smidgen of mocking, so as not to scare him away from the two things that make him such a national treasure: a podium and a microphone.

Thus, as our nation's electorate begins to make the tough choices of what to do on election day next year instead of voting, we promise to be fair and measured in any criticism we may have of the man who for four years didn't know how to spell "potato." (Hint: one "p.")

Specifically, we promise that for every time we make fun of Dan Quayle we'll also make fun of another candidate.

Okay, how about this: For every three times we poke fun at Dan Quayle...actually, this could be more difficult than I thought. Unless Lamar "The Shirt" Alexander proves once again that he can answer the really tough political questions, such as: "Lamar who?"

IN FAIRNESS to Dan Quayle's election bid, it must be said that not everyone is laughing at the idea. In fact, Republican leaders have been enthusiastic about Quayle's candidacy and have promised their party's full support, just as soon as monkeys fly.

To his credit, Quayle has already announced a decisive and hard-hitting approach to governing. He has pledged that the day he takes office he would immediately call for the impeachment and removal of the president, thus bringing a merciful end to our national nightmare.

So let the campaign begin. I can't waite. ∎

An Advent Meditation

(Editor's Note: To best understand how George W. Bush be-came our president let's look back before the early primaries of 1999, when his candidacy—much less two terms as president—was very much in question. The following was written that sum-mer for the December deadline of Sojourners magazine, a pro-gressive Christian publication that just can't help but put Jesus in everything, even politics. We join a reading of the Christmas narrative from the New Testament book of Matthew, already in progress.)

And lo (or, depending on your translation, "yo"), an an-gel of the Lord appeared before the shepherds tending their flocks by night and, despite enormous temptation, did not sneak RIGHT up on them and shout "BOO!" What the angel actually said was, "Behold, unto you a child is born, unto you a son is given." But the shepherds were either sore or afraid, for lo, they realized that this was both good news and bad news. The good news was that God had finally decided to speak to them. The bad news was they didn't understand a word of it.

FIRST SHEPHERD: Do you know what that angel just said?

SECOND SHEPHERD: No. But it sounded like 17th-centu-ry English.

FIRST SHEPHERD: But that can't be, since the English are still just a bunch of un-evolved Druids who pray to anything they can't eat. Also, they smell bad. Talk about clearing out a tent.

SECOND SHEPHERD: Hmmm...I wonder if my in-laws are Druids.

FIRST SHEPHERD: He's still standing over there.

SECOND SHEPHERD: Who?

FIRST SHEPHERD: That angel guy. And he keeps saying "lo."

SECOND SHEPHERD: Let's ignore him and maybe he'll go away.

FIRST SHEPHERD: Anyway, as I was saying before the angel showed up, I'm sick of tending our flocks by night. Any idea how to get back on the day shift?

OH WHAT'S the use? I can't write inspirational Christmas stuff now, even though you depend on me for that sort of thing. But it's 90 degrees in Washington, D.C. and it's August (note redundancy) just like it always is for the December deadline. We're in Heat Hell but have to write about the hope of Advent. I don't think so.

And it's even harder this time since I just got back from our annual drive-till-we-drop vacation to the West (motto: You're not there yet). And folks out West weren't talking about Christmas. They were talking about more immediate concerns, such as how to spell "Albuquerque" and wondering what George W. Bush hasn't done in the last 23 years.

The Iowa straw polls took place while I was in the area (actually I was a thousand miles away, but out West that's considered close), and I was able to observe history in the making. Okay, the purchase of history in the making.

You probably heard that George W. did well in these polls. The question that hasn't been answered, however, is "Fine. But who is this guy?" He could be the next president of the United States and the only thing I know about George W. Bush is what he didn't do and won't deny. (That's what I like about Bill Clinton: You know exactly what he did because he denies he ever did it. Which means of course he did it.)

Given the amount of campaign contributions he's already raised, Bush looked like a shoe-in for being voted highest bidder for the presidency, but then something bad happened. Or, to quote fellow candidate Steve Forbes, "Oh GOODY!"

Things turned sour for Bush when journalists who used drugs in college demanded to know if he did too. The second question they asked was if he could spare some, but that didn't make it to broadcast.

The other Republican hopefuls saw a talking point and quickly assured the American people that they had never used drugs, mainly because they never lived in my dorm. Dan Quayle pointed out that he had never used drugs, or a dictionary, in his entire life, but then got distracted by "some weird guy staring at me with a wild look in his eyes." When told that person was Steve Forbes and that's how he looks at everybody, Dan Quayle said, presidentially, "Oh."

The results of the Iowa straw poll were, in order of most money...I mean most votes:

1. George W. Bush
2. Steve Forbes
3. Elizabeth Dole
4. A bunch of other people.
5. Somebody else.
6. Dan Quayle

As you can see, Dan Quayle fared the worst in the straw poll. In fact, 90 percent of straw polled admitted that, even if they were registered, they would not vote for him. Quayle is currently having his official portrait taken for use on the sides of milk cartons.

And speaking of Lamar Alexander, after his own poor

showing he was awarded the coveted prize of first Iowa Carcass of the political season. He's dropping out of politics altogether and returning to the lonely and pitiable life of a retired multimillionaire.

Elizabeth Dole, who has yet to deny that her husband used Viagra when he was in college, credited her unexpectedly strong third place showing to an "invisible army" of voters. However, she failed to explain why, if she had an invisible army, she didn't place first or, for that matter, just take over the whole process. When you have an invisible army you can pretty much do what you want.

Heck, if I had an invisible army I'd do something way more cool than run for president. I'd go over to the potato chip factory and throw my weight around: "ATTENTION IN THERE: YOU ARE SURROUNDED BY AN INVISIBLE ARMY! WE DEMAND YOU MAKE ONLY SALT 'N' VINEGAR CHIPS! AND DO IT NOW, OR ELSE!"

"What? Well of course you can't see them. THEY'RE INVISIBLE!"

Al Gore wishes he had an invisible army (although I've heard he has an imaginary friend), instead of a team of high-priced advisers who, in a brilliant stroke of political savvy, urged the vice president to move his entire campaign headquarters to Nashville, Tennessee. This was done in the hope of reminding the voters of that state that, before spending almost his entire life in the nation's capitol, attending the most exclusive private schools and growing up as the son of a U.S. Senator, he was briefly born in Tennessee. ∎

Shecky Boaz:
First Century Comedian

Archaeologists carefully studying the ancient Dead Sea Scrolls have discovered a lengthy passage that had been previously overlooked and un-translated. Scientists believe the document is a transcript from a one-man show at a Judean night club 2,000 years ago. Following, in its entirety, is the translation titled simply:

Shecky Boaz: First-Century Comedian

Thank you. Thank you very much. It's great to be here. I just walked in from Tyre, and so are my feet. Hey but I had a good time up there—you know those wacky northern beach towns. Fun-loving folks, but as for intelligence, well, I think they're only fishing from one side of the boat, if you know what I mean.

But seriously, ladies and gentlemen, it's great to be back at Bethlehem's Chez Caesar, the best night club in Judea. And I should know, I've played some real dumps in my time, from Sidon to Nicopolis. And I stunk up the place once in Arimathea, but hey, I don't want to talk about it.

But nobody, and I mean this sincerely, nobody gives me as warm a welcome as you guys...I said nobody gives me as warm a...thank you, thank you very much.

And speaking of taxes—and who doesn't speak of taxes in Bethlehem?—isn't that Zacchaeus in the back there? Yes it is Zacchaeus, the Zacchster, the Zacchmeister, Baron von Big Guy.

Stand up, Zacch, so we can...oh, you are standing up. Sorry about that. Hah, hah! Just kidding. Say, is that your oxcart parked outside, the one with the "Render Unto Caesar" bumper sticker? I thought so. Not that I mind paying Caesar 80 percent of my wages. Hey, I love the guy. You know, Caesar and I have this understanding: I pay my taxes, and he lets me live. Which reminds me—what's the difference between a tax collector and a centurion? The centurion only sticks you once.

And speaking of centurions, I think I see a couple of Rome's finest out in the audience. Welcome to the club, boys, nice outfits. But where'd you get those ugly helmets? What's that? You're not wearing helmets? Oops. My mistake. But seriously, I love these guys, and they must be tired. Persecuting unarmed civilians is an exhausting full-time job.

But I hear that some centurions are having a little trouble with their new chariots. Well guys, let me give you a hint: The horses go in front.

Ouch, that smarts. Not that centurions are dumb or anything, but I heard that some of them are paying rabbis to take their entrance exams.

Sorry guys. Guess it's been a rough week, what with the escape and all. But give me a break. How hard is it to guard a tomb, huh? And with a big stone in front of it? I wish I could have been there when you reported THAT to the boss. But cheer up fellows. If you're lucky, you won't get the John the Baptist haircut, if you know what I mean.

And speaking of the boss, isn't that Pontius Pilate coming out of the men's room? Yo, Pontius! Washing your hands again? Ha ha! Ooh, look at the scowl on his face. Say what? You could have me beheaded? Heh, I'm dyin' up here already, Mr. P., so who needs the help?

But seriously folks, we love our governor, don't we? Nobody, and I mean nobody, grovels before the Emperor like our Pontius. It's a real gift. And speaking of the Emperor, and I mean this sincerely, Caesar is the kindest, warmest, most compassionate man I have ever known. I can repeat that if the Scribes in the back didn't get it all.

Say, did you hear about Barabbas? Yeah, he was arrested again. They booked him for grand theft donkey. And have you heard about the new scam the Sadducees are running over at the temple? Something called "bingo." The church folks love it, I hear, and the winners get discounts at the sacrificial meat counter.

And speaking of the temple, what day is complete without a condescending scowl from one of our great interpreters of the law, the Pharisees? Nothing brightens up the Sabbath like being flogged for bending over to pick up something you dropped.

Which reminds me, I heard that Satan once offered unlimited wealth, power, and fame to a Pharisee in return for his soul. The Pharisee replied: "Sounds good to me. What's the catch?"

And do you know how to tell a Pharisee from a poisonous snake? Me neither.

Hey, well, I see my time is up. But it's been great, and as my lute player Raheeb starts my theme song I can only say: You must remember this, a kiss is just a kiss, a scythe is just a scythe, the fundamental things apply, PAY YOUR TAXES AND BE GOOD TO EACH OTHER...GOOD NIGHT EVERYBODY! ∎

APPENDIX 4

A Calendar to Set Your Clock By

July is a special month. And not just because it's the birth month of our nation, which was inaugurated in 1776 when Benjamin Franklin, having already invented the iPod, introduced the hot dog, which George Washington ate two of, and in the process triggered our young nation's first commemorative case of acid reflux.

July is also the last month of summer in which a cool breeze can still surprise you on a busy street, drying the sweat off your face as you stand on the corner considering whether to wait for the light or, in the stubbornly independent spirit of our nation, boldly cross against the light, evoking the proud motto of New Hampshire: "Live Free or Die Under a Bus." The chance of a breeze ends quickly come August, however, when the oppressive heat reminds us that our planet is slowly boiling itself to death and our only hope is in prayers and service to a merciful God.

But thankfully we don't have to do those things now, because July is also the second full month of Ordinary Time, the period on the Catholic liturgical calendar that is free of religious obligation and ritual. Unlike the other seasons—Advent, Lent, Epiphany, Pentecost, and, if memory serves, Eureka—Ordinary Time requires little from practicing Christians: no sacrifice or acts of charity, no special offerings, no tedious Christmas shopping lists. Nope. Just a few weeks for kicking back and doing something ordinary, like having a cold beverage. For the church, it's Miller Time.

Before you correct the point, I realize that in this case the word "ordinary" derives from the term ordinal or "numbered," signifying that the Sundays in this period are not necessarily ordinary, but are simply numbered. But hey, don't blame me if the early church fathers decided to knock off during the summer. Frankly, as one who is searching for just the right spiritual balance in life, a church-sanctioned season where you and God just, you know, hit a volleyball back and forth is just what this former Baptist has been waiting for.

BAPTISTS HAVE traditionally been skeptical of some Catholic practices, particularly infant baptism, since we feel that to fully comprehend a lifetime of Christian service one must first reach an age of maturity, say about 10; 11 at the outside. Not to mention another big point of tension, what some have characterized as steeple envy, which Baptists often suffer from. (Catholic churches always have bells. We never had bells. I like bells.)

Admittedly, Baptists are themselves pretty weak on religious ritual, unless you count Super Bowl Sunday, which we fully honor with sermons that mine football's rich allegorical trove: "And Jesus said: 'Down. Ready set. Go ye therefore and teach all nations ... .' "

Occasionally, though, in the small town of my youth, Catholics and Baptists would reach across the theological divide and work together to solve the pressing spiritual issues of our small town. Namely, finding a power forward for our church basketball team. For some reason, Baptists can't produce good power forwards. (Backward we're good at, but not forward.) Fortunately, the Catholic church down the street always had extra, most of whom were tired of ringing the church bells as part of their weekly obligation. So they gladly became temporary Baptists, and they didn't seem to mind taking our sacramental grape juice—or Hawaiian Punch, depending on what was left from Vacation Bible School—and then crossing themselves from right to left. Then, after we forgave them their pope, they went out and practiced free throws.

ORDINARY TIME IS ALSO a good time to atone for little mistakes made in other seasons. For example, during this past Lent—a time of spiritual cleansing and soul-searching—the Defense Department accidentally shipped ballistic missile parts to Taiwan. The shipment was supposed to contain helicopter batteries, but because of an error made somewhere along the supply line, it didn't. It was ballistic missile parts.

No judgment here. It was an honest mistake, and what better time to make it than during a season of confession and self-examination. (And let them without sin cast the first spare part.) Why, just last week I myself walked out of the grocery store with a case of weapons-grade uranium that I thought was Chex Mix (in the Bold Party Flavor!). Fortunately, the security guard noticed my mistake when his heart pacemaker started playing a local radio station. And, since I still had the receipt, I had no problem exchanging it for cans of tuna laced with heavy metals, for which I had suddenly developed a taste.

But all good things must end, which Ordinary Time does in November with the Feast of Christ the King, followed, I would imagine, by the Second Helping of Dessert for the King, which consists mainly of snickerdoodles, a cinnamon sugar cookie that, it turns out, you can eat 37 of before you realize what a bad idea it was. (When Lent comes around, I'm really hoping I remember that, because giving them up would make an excellent Lenten discipline. These liturgical seasons have real promise.) ∎

Wrongs and Rites of Passage

Throughout history, humans have lived within the context of patterns: patterns of behavior, movement, language, and weekly TV sitcoms ("Thursdays are Must-See TV on NBC!"). Within more organized societies some patterns have been formalized into rituals used to shepherd young people into adulthood. Of course, we aren't talking about the common, everyday rituals that all of us have, such as turning around in a circle exactly nine times before brushing your teeth, or carefully folding your napkin in an inward-facing triangle that slightly overlaps the left edge of your plate. Normal as these practices are, they are not the transformative moments of a young man's life. (They're more in the category of minor compulsions that I freely admit to and which I could stop anytime I wanted if my therapist WOULD JUST STOP *HARPING* ABOUT IT!)

No, the rituals to which I refer are the rites of passage, the moments of testing and preparation that, unfortunately, have been lost in our society because of the high level of fluoride in our drinking water.

A number of us first heard Father Richard Rohr share these ideas (except the part about the fluoride) in a weekend retreat last year and we were deeply moved by his presentation. I was especially touched when, sensing that I had a more intuitive understanding than the other participants, he took me aside and quietly but firmly said, "Don't you *dare* make fun of this. in that stupid column of your!"

It must be said that Father Rohr is a quiet, soft-spoken Franciscan priest who doesn't usually press his face up so close that you can feel the imprint of his rosary on your chest. But for me he made an exception, and as I cowered before him I realized how foolish I must have appeared. It doesn't look good to be intimidated by a Franciscan. Jesuits are a little scary, of course, and who could blame you for crossing the street to avoid a bunch of Capuchins hanging out on the corner. But nobody's supposed to get pushed around by a Franciscan. (Although, in fairness to me, this particular priest was wearing a pair of "Born-to-Raise-Hell" sandals. And I had heard that he occasionally gets testy during the liturgy and says stuff like "What's this 'also with you' business? I'm talkin' here! Do you want a piece of me? Do I amuse you?!")

Alas, this episode was just another reminder of my own pitifully inadequate rites of passage when I was young. I remember them all:

There was the annual Christmas Pageant at my church, where, year after year, I was ritually passed over for the part of Joseph. This rejection taught me at an early age to accept failure and lowered expectations. It also showed me how to be a shepherd, in case I ever got a job doing that. (Actually, it's not so hard, since you basically just stand next to the pulpit wearing your father's bathrobe and a dish towel around your head.)

There was also my baptism in the Southern Baptist church where I emerged from the water of life free from sin, but with really bad hair. (This moment was made even more awkward as I dripped and spluttered in the baptistery and gazed out at my young friends in the pews who were desperately clamping their hands over their mouths so as not to vocalize their "expressions of enormous respect," as my mother later explained.)

Or the day my shop teacher replied to a timid inquiry from me: "There are no stupid questions, Mr. Spivey. Just stupid people, like you." (This rebuke was especially hard to take since we were in awe of this man. He was the only teacher who taught us anything we could actually use in later life; specifically, how to make an ashtray and how to not punch a hole in your hand with a drill press.)

To be truthful, there were times when I was clearly being called out of my youth and into the tentative first steps of manhood. I'll never forget the thrill of recognition one Sunday when the preacher called me aside—much like a Catholic priest confers with the altar boy before Mass—and gave me the important task of telling the deacons they should "put out their blasted cigarettes and get back inside, for crying out loud" since it was almost time for church. (Baptists of the 1950s believed that people were better prepared for worship if they first passed through the sacred "Cloud of Veranda Smoke" that was dutifully prepared for them by the men of the church.)

And I just knew I had arrived at adulthood the first time a hardware store employee laughed at my poor choice of tools. "You see this, fella. This here's a crescent wrench. You don't need a crescent wrench to change that little light bulb in your refrigerator!" He wouldn't have talked like that to a boy. No way.

DESPITE these impressive milestones, however, I can never overcome my biggest failure as a young man. A failure that forced me to watch as countless of my peers rose to the rank of Eagle Scout without me because I refused to memorize the all-important tool of the prepared American male: Morse code. (I figured, when am I ever going to need this?)

I still have nightmares about being trapped in an old telegraph office surrounded by a band of taunting outlaws. They ride their horses back and forth laughing loudly and waving their cellphones in the air as my frightened family crouches in a corner, watching me, waiting for me to call for help using the only device on hand: an ancient telegraph.

But I can't. I can only curse a Boy Scout career that resulted in just one accomplishment: a merit badge in cooking. With no one to blame but myself, I tap out what I vaguely remember is the universal distress signal: SO4...No, that's not right. SUS... Darn! How about S2O? But it sounds like gibberish to the operator in a nearby town, and he eventually dismisses it as just another teen-age Morse code prank.

CLEARLY, rites of passage are important, and if I had a son I would look forward to the moment in his life when I would take him into the woods where he would stay alone for 24 hours. Using only his wits and a small penknife, his task would be to open a shrink-wrapped compact disc. He has to know how to do this to be a man.

And when he has learned, maybe he can teach me. ∎

Back from Camp

We're looking at photos from our daughters' summer camps. Here's a picture of our 14-year-old smiling with friends at the lake, a picture with her clowning for the camera in her bedroom, and another with her hugging a horse named "Butterscotch".

Our 16-year-old went to a different camp. Here's a picture of her at the back of a canoe, cold and soaked, saying something harsh ("oh fiddlesticks," perhaps, but I can't be sure). In another picture she is in a body harness, unsmiling and determined, at the base of a seven-story cliff. And lots of photos that didn't turn out since, she explained, there's not much light in caves.

Two different camps, two very different experiences. Kate, our youngest daughter, came back talking about how fun it was to meet new friends, sing camp songs and roast marshmallows. Our older daughter, Colleen, came back...a ninja.

WHEN WE BEGAN looking for good summer activities we particularly wanted Colleen, our oldest, to have a vigorous outdoor experience, since she was recovering from corrective surgery to both legs and needed to get back her muscle tone and strength. She did.

Her camp—which we'll call "Lord of the Flies Camp"— could not have contrasted more with Kate's—which we'll call Camp Britney Spears. Her camp was a Fun Camp, with dorm rooms, cafeteria meals, sing-a-longs, campfires, and canoeing.

Colleen's camp had canoes and campfires, too. But the fires were for drying out from the canoeing ("It was okay, Dad. It only rained for three days" on their three-day canoe trip.) And there were few marshmallows. "We don't do a lot of marshmallows here," the counselor had said when I dropped her off. He was a stone-lean young man with unwavering eyes and a painful handshake whom we'll call... "Snake."

Our youngest daughter's counselors were Missy and Christy.

To continue the comparisons, Kate's camp has a beautiful main lodge, with lovely outbuildings, a nearby lake, and tennis courts.

Colleen's camp has tents. Just tents. In the vernacular of realtors, her camp "doesn't show well." In fact, the first impression left me wondering why we spent the nearly a thousand dollars on what looked to be an abandoned mining camp. "Don't worry, sir" said another counselor (whom we'll call ..."Rock"), who seemed a little annoyed when I muttered something about the cost. "Your daughter will earn every penny of it."

We should have suspected the differences when we first read the registration materials. "Don't forget your tennis racket!" Kate's camp brochure enthused, exclamation points being the punctuation of choice.

"Bring good socks," the other brochure stated.

We didn't figure out the rest until after the girls returned, but perhaps this was better since "you would have worried," suggested our oldest. Their letters from camp contained little by way of detail, although in hindsight our oldest daughter's had clues: her two postcards were wet and torn, with something that might have been hand-writing scrawled across one side. We were able to decipher "rattlesnake in tent—gotta go."

It turns out that while our 14-year-old was having her first sailing lesson on a quiet lake, our 16-year-old was starting that exhausting canoe trip down the Shenandoah River. As mentioned, it rained a lot. When it rained at our youngest daughter's camp they played board games inside. When it rained on the other group they just kept going—six hours a day over rocks and around logs—until early evening when they dragged their canoes ashore and set up camp. In the rain. They also started a fire in the rain and ate in the rain. And slept—sort of—in the rain.

To be truthful, our oldest daughter wasn't outdoors the whole time. After the canoe trip she went into caves. And not the kind of caves we parents like—with lights and walkways and a snack bar at the end. These were crawl-in-and-be-scared caves. The kind of cave where you reach out in the dark and touch the bones of a hapless 19th-century wanderer who, wounded and frightened, had CRAWLED IN THERE TO DIE!

Not to project my own fears. ("You wouldn't have made it, Dad.")

While our youngest daughter was playing tennis at her camp, her sister was crawling a hundred yards into a dark, narrow tunnel. She wasn't scared, she claimed, "just cold." The water in the cave—a not-quite-summerish 50 degrees—was about eight inches deep, not so bad if you're walking through it. But she was crawling on her belly. "I didn't mind so much," she said, "until my lamp went out. Then you couldn't see the bats. You just felt them." Bats sleep during the day but, it turns out, they wake up when you brush against them with your head.

Kate slept indoors in a warm bed. The only time Colleen even used the word "warm" was to observe out loud one night, to no one in particular, that she "forgot what warm feels like."

At Kate's camp, they held hands in a circle and sang. They didn't sing much at the other camp, but they held hands real tight on a foot-wide ledge next to a two-story drop-off. This was in another cave. At least they had their leader's reassurance that it was "only a few more yards" until they could rise from the crouching position they'd been in for over an hour. And then Colleen's light went out again.

OUR YOUNGEST DAUGHTER loved the horseback riding, and gave frequent hugs to her favorite horse, "Butterscotch." Our oldest daughter didn't name the animals they discovered during their cross-country hikes (with full pack). Nor did she hug them, since snakes and skunks aren't the hugging sort.

Kate played table tennis with her new friends. Colleen climbed over a 100-foot cliff with hers, and then rappelled down the other side. "We had safety lines, Dad." (So they could easily pull up the bodies?)

Kate took a side trip to a nearby miniature golf course ("I made two holes-in-one!"). Colleen made a hole in her life jacket when she fell out of the raft in Level Five white-water rapids. "It's okay. I only fell out twice."

Our youngest daughter had meat and vegetables (and a roll) at most meals. Our oldest daughter ate mainly carbohydrates for energy, and no meat, since the smell would attract animals. On the other hand, if they had attracted a large animal "maybe it would have kept the snakes away. That would have been nice."

Kate ate on plates with knives and forks and napkins. Colleen was issued a plastic bowl and a spoon. Her camp teaches "minimum environmental impact," which means they don't waste water and they don't waste food. While our 14-year-old was carrying her plate back to the kitchen to be washed by the staff, our other daughter was sitting on a tree stump, scraping out the last bite of food from her bowl. Then, as instructed by stern counselors, she swished her bowl "clean" with a little water. And then she drank the water.

"Gross!" Kate cringed when she heard.

"It's what you do in the wilderness," Colleen calmly explained.

One daughter had a hot shower every night. The other one washed, let's just say, less often.

The most asked question at Kate's camp: "What's for dessert tonight?"

At Colleen's camp: "Can we rest for awhile?" ("No.")

At the end of camp our youngest said tearful farewells to her new friends and to her horse ("Butterscotch"). Our oldest daughter helped clean out the latrine. It was hard work but "you get used to hard work." Now I *knew* this camp was a good idea. Either that, or we got back somebody else's kid.

Kate returned home with the addresses of her new friends. Colleen came back with cuts too numerous too mention, but she mentioned them anyway, one by one, since each had its own story. "But, they look a lot better now," she assured us as we inspected her wounds. She also had bruises ("I was hanging upside down from a rope and wham! somebody accidentally let go. Hah! Hah!"), and dozens of lacerations on her lower legs. These were from a game called "Instinct," which helps the players become one with nature, specifically the parts of nature that have sharp edges: thorns, rocks, and scratchy bark. "We loved it," she reported with a big smile. "By the way, is this our only bottle of rubbing alcohol?"

As parents we have no complaints. Our 14-year-old had the kind of fun a girl her age should have. And our 16-year-old had, well, the kind of fun Marines have. Our oldest daughter is proud of her cuts and bruises, and her green fatigues "with lots of pockets for gear." (She had never used the word "gear" before.) She is stronger, more determined, more confident and proud of what she accomplished.

Now they resume their lives, return to school and to normal children's activities, such as making Christmas lists: Our 14-year-old wants makeup, a computer game, and some new CDs.

Our 16-year-old just wants a knife. A big knife. ∎